HISTORY REVISION NOTES
FOR
JUNIOR CERTIFICATE

Desmond O'Leary

Gill & Macmill

GW00777684

Gill & Macmillan Ltd
Hume Avenue
Park West
Dublin 12
with associated companies throughout the world
www.gillmacmillan.ie
© Desmond O'Leary 1994, 2000
© Artwork Gill & Macmillan 1994, 2000
0 7171 3022 3
Design and Artwork by Paul McElheron & Associates, Dublin
Print origination by Paul McElheron & Associates, Dublin

The paper used in this book is made from the wood pulp of managed forests.
For every tree felled, at least one tree is planted, thereby renewing natural resources.

Contents

PHOTO RESEARCH: Anne-Marie Ehrlich
ILLUSTRATIONS: Brian O'Halloran (Jerpoint Abbey and Kells); D. Newman Johnson (Trim Castle).
PHOTOS: Office of Public Works; Cambridge University; British Museum; Robert Harding Picture Library; A.F. Kersting; Photographie Giraudon; Ulster Museum, Photographie Bulloz; Hulton-Deutsch Collection; National Museum of Ireland; Mansell Collection; Pacemaker; Keystone; Connacht Tribune; British Library.

1 INTRODUCTION

HISTORY

A. What is History?
1. The English word 'history' comes from the Greek word 'historia', which means story.
2. 'History' is therefore the story of the past told as truthfully as possible.

B. Evidence
1. History is based on evidence, i.e. on material that remains from the past.
2. Sometimes evidence is in the form of objects, e.g. coins, buildings or pictures.
3. However, historians are especially interested in documentary (written) evidence.
4. Written evidence consists of primary and secondary sources.
5. Primary sources were written by people directly involved in an event, e.g. a diary, a battle report, an eyewitness newspaper account.
6. Secondary sources were written by people not directly involved in an event, e.g. a school textbook.

C. Problems
1. We cannot always be certain about history.
2. Sources may have been destroyed, e.g. during the Civil War in Ireland.
3. Sources may also be inaccurate: anyone involved in an event will tell the story mainly from his or her own point of view.
4. Some historians who feel very strongly about a subject may at times deliberately mislead their readers.

PREHISTORY

A. Prehistory
The word 'prehistory' refers to the time before writing was invented.

B. Archaeology
1. Our knowledge of prehistory depends mainly on archaeology.
2. Archaeologists try to find out about prehistoric people by examining material excavated from the ground.

C. Finding a Site
1. Some sites are well known long before they are excavated, e.g. Troy and Tara.
2. An interesting site may be discovered by accident.
3. Aerial photography may reveal a site not visible at ground level.

D. Excavating a Site

An archaeologist excavates a site according to set procedures.

1. First, he or she makes a detailed map of the area.
2. Next, the area is divided into grids, which are marked on the map.
3. Then, very carefully, he or she digs out each grid using trowels, brushes and sieves.
4. Each find is recorded on the map.
5. Cross-sections are drawn to show the depth at which each object was found.
6. Each object is sketched and photographed.
7. All the information about the finds is recorded on a card index.
8. The age of each find is calculated.

E. Dating Objects

Archaeological remains can be dated as follows.

1. Stratigraphy: the higher an object is in a series of layers, the younger it is; the deeper it is, the older it is.
2. Carbon 14 dating measures the age of organic material, e.g. clothes, timber, human remains, by counting the number of neutrons in its carbon atoms.
3. Dendrochronology is used to date timber objects, e.g. ships or buildings, by counting their tree rings and comparing their patterns with those of known age.

F. Archaeology and Science

Other scientific methods are used to help archaeologists.

1. Pollen analysis tells them what plants grew in an area. This indicates what kind of farming, if any, was carried on.
2. Bones tell archaeologists what animals were kept by the inhabitants of a site. In the case of human remains, bones will tell the archaeologists about people's diseases and their age at death.
3. By analysing the mineral content of pots and other objects, archaeologists can get an idea of where the raw materials came from and therefore they learn about trade routes, etc.
4. Forensic scientists can reconstruct the appearance of ancient people from their remains, e.g. the head of Lindown man who was murdered about two thousand years ago has been reconstructed from remains found in a Cheshire bog.

The remains of Lindown man found in a Cheshire Bog

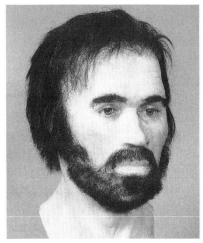

A scientific reconstruction of Lindown man's appearance

2 PREHISTORIC IRELAND

THE EARLIEST SETTLERS

A. End of the Ice Age
1. Huge ice-caps covered Ireland during the last ice age.
2. By c. 8000 BC most of the ice had melted and animals and mesolithic (middle stone age) hunters entered the island, probably using land bridges linking Ireland with Britain and the Continent.

B. Mount Sandel
1. The oldest known site used by these hunters is at Mount Sandel, near the River Bann.
2. Archaeologists digging there discovered animal and fish bones, pollen, microliths, post holes and the remains of fires.

C. How the People Lived
This evidence tells us much about the 'Sandelians'.
1. They hunted deer and wild pigs in forests of oak and elm.
2. They fished for salmon and eels.
3. They ate wild berries and nuts.
4. They made scrapers, punches and arrowheads from flint obtained in Antrim.
5. The Sandelians built dome-shaped huts consisting of a framework of branches covered with thatch or skins.

Prehistoric Ireland

6. The site at Mount Sandel was occupied *c. 7000–6500 BC.*
7. No human remains were found at Mount Sandel. We do not know what the people looked like. We do not know what language they spoke, where they came from or why they abandoned their site.

FARMERS AND BUILDERS

A. The Evidence
1. Neolithic (new stone age) farmers entered Ireland about 3500 BC.
2. Finds of bones show that they kept cattle, sheep and pigs.
3. Pollen indicates that they grew wheat and barley.
4. Excavations at Belderg, Co. Mayo show that they (i) divided the fertile land into walled fields and (ii) used cultivation ridges similar to modern 'lazy beds'.

B. Artifacts
1. These farmers also made clay pots in which they kept their grain and seed and in which they cooked their food.
2. Their tools and weapons were better than those of the hunters and included large, polished stone axes with which they cleared the land of trees.

C. Houses

1. Excavations at Lough Gur, Co. Limerick show that these farmers lived in large circular or rectangular houses built from sods of earth piled on stone foundations and covered with a thatched roof.
2. Some houses had wickerwork walls plastered with mud.
3. These huts were easily built. They were warm in winter and cool in summer.
4. However, they must have been dark, dirty and smoke-filled.
5. They were also very similar to houses found in many parts of Ireland until recently!

D. The Tombs

1. Neolithic farmers built megalithic (enormous stone) tombs. These included: court cairns, dolmens, wedge tombs and passage graves.
2. Court cairns, e.g. at Ballyglass, Co. Mayo, consist of (i) a long, narrow corridor of stone uprights divided by jambs and lintels into separate compartments, (ii) covered with a mound of pebbles and stones and with a circular court to the front. (iii) Archaeologists believe that bodies were cremated in the court and that the ashes and bones were placed in the cairn.
3. Dolmens, e.g. at Kilclooney, Co. Donegal, (i) consist of three uprights and a capstone. (ii) Cremated remains were buried beneath a pot in the centre of the dolmen and (iii) the entire structure was then covered with a mound of stones.

Kilclooney dolmen. When first completed, this structure was covered with a mound of earth and stones

4. Wedge tombs, e.g. at Lough Gur, consist of a chamber, low and narrow at one end, high and broad at the other, with a small porch.
5. Passage graves, e.g. at Newgrange and Knowth, consist of (i) a long, narrow passage leading into a (ii) cross-shaped chamber with a (iii) high corbelled roof over the central part. (iv) The passage and chamber were then covered with a huge mound bordered with intricately carved stones.
6. At Newgrange the rising sun on the winter solstice shines directly along the passage to illuminate the back wall of the tomb.

7. This obvious connection with astronomy has caused many archaeologists to wonder whether Newgrange was built as a temple or as an observatory and only later used as a tomb.

The central corbelled chamber of the passage grave at Newgrange showing the famous triple spiral and entrance

THE BRONZE AGE

A. The Beaker People

About 2000 BC the Beaker People (named after a type of pot associated with them) settled in Ireland and apparently introduced bronze-making.

B. Bronze

1. Bronze is an alloy (mixture) of tin and copper.
2. Copper occurs in Ireland and archaeologists have excavated ancient copper mines at Mount Gabriel near Bantry.
3. However, tin had to be imported and this indicates that Ireland had regular contact with tin-producing areas in Europe.
4. Smiths smelted the ores to extract the pure tin and copper.
5. The metals were then mixed and poured into moulds to produce spearheads, arrowheads, axes, swords and daggers.
6. The swords and daggers indicate that warfare was becoming common in Ireland and this is confirmed by finds of wooden shields covered with leather and studded with bronze.

C. A Golden Age

1. The Bronze Age was also a golden age.
2. Alluvial gold from Co. Wicklow was made into sun-discs, lunulae and bracelets.
3. Many of these were exported, possibly to pay for tin.

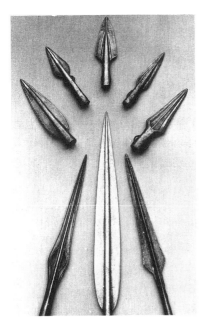

Bronze Age spearheads

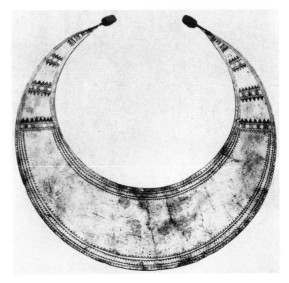

Lunula found near Lough Ree in Co. Westmeath.
It dates from c. 1800 BC

D. Buildings

1. New kinds of buildings were constructed for defence during the Bronze Age. These included raths, caiseals, promontory forts, hillforts and crannogs.
2. A rath or ringfort consisted of a circular earthen and timber wall surrounded by a ditch.
3. Raths contained huts and cattle pens and many had souterrains, i.e. stone-lined tunnels, probably used for storage.
4. Caiseals were similar to ringforts but were built from stone, e.g. Staigue Fort and Grianán Aileach.
5. Promontory forts were headlands protected by steep cliffs towards the sea and by man-made walls towards the land.
6. Thus Dún Aenghus on Inishmore is protected by sheer cliffs and by three concentric walls interspersed with a *chevaux de frise*, i.e. sharp stones tilted to hamper attackers.
7. A crannog was an artificial island with houses and walls built in a lake. Such islands were usually small and difficult to build and were probably places of refuge rather than normal places of settlement. Important finds were discovered at Lagore crannog in Co. Meath.

E. Stone Circles

1. Bronze Age people also built stone circles, e.g. at Drombeg, Co. Cork.
2. These may have been used as astronomical observatories or temples or burial grounds.

Dún Aenghus promontory fort. Note the triple walls and the chevaux de frise in the foreground

Replica of a crannog, Craggaunowen, Co. Clare

F. Fulacht Fiadh

1. Fulacht fiadh were used to cook meat. They were large stone- or timber-lined pits filled with water.
2. Hot stones were then tossed into the water. When the water was hot, meat wrapped in straw was thrown in and was kept submerged until cooked.

THE CELTS

A. Origins

1. The Celts originated in central Europe and gradually migrated until they occupied most of Europe.
2. However, the Celts did not form a great political empire like the Romans.
3. Each tribe was independent but they were linked by similar languages, customs, laws, religions and traditions.
4. Because they failed to unite, the European Celts were easily overwhelmed by the Romans.
5. Celtic society survived much longer in Ireland but it too was eventually overcome by the better-organised English.

B. Settlement

1. Celts first entered Ireland about 600 BC. The last groups arrived about the time of Christ.
2. Some groups travelled directly from mainland Europe while others came through Britain.
3. The Celts were Europe's finest ironworkers and their iron weapons enabled them to overwhelm the earlier bronze-using peoples.

C. The Tuatha

1. Celtic Ireland consisted of many tiny kingdoms called tuatha.
2. Each tuath had its own rí (king) who was elected from and by a group of close relations called a deirbhfhine.
3. Disputed elections often caused civil wars and sometimes led to the establishment of new tuatha.
4. According to Celtic (Brehon) law no man could be rí if he were disfigured. This often encouraged ambitious men to mutilate rivals.
5. Sometimes, a rí would arrange for a tánaiste (successor) to be elected during his lifetime to avoid such conflicts.
6. Once in power, the rí had to look after his tuath, to defend it against its enemies, to lead his warriors on raids and to see that his people were treated justly.

D. Social Classes

1. Each tuath contained distinct social classes.
2. There was the king and his family who controlled the land.
3. They let out the land to farmers who were freemen and who paid rent in cattle and food.
4. The warriors and farmers had slaves to do the heavy work.
5. There were also craftsmen such as smiths, carpenters and metalworkers.
6. The Aos Dána or learned classes were very important.
7. They included brehons (judges), filí (poets), doctors and historians.
8. Members of the Aos Dána spent a long time training at special schools.
9. They learned by heart all the lore of their professions. Celts did not write down information in case the manuscripts got lost and nobody remembered what had been written.
10. The Aos Dána were highly regarded and travelled freely from tuath to tuath in search of the best-paid employment.
11. The filí were especially important and were much feared.
12. If a king displeased them, they could cause him great embarrassment by composing satires (mocking poems) about him.
13. However, they heaped praise on rulers who paid them well.

E. Appearance

1. The Celts took great care of their appearance.
2. They washed frequently and bleached and styled their hair carefully so that it swept back from their foreheads and hung in long ringlets down the back of their necks.
3. The men wore long moustaches and these seem to have got in the way when they were eating and drinking.

F. Clothes

1. The Celts wore very colourful woollen clothes, often decorated with check patterns.
2. Men and women alike wore long tunics and the men also wore long trousers, strapped to the leg below the knee.
3. They also wore large cloaks which served as a blanket when they slept and as a tent when they travelled.

G. Food and Drink

1. The Celts in Ireland were mainly involved in cattle-rearing.
2. Their animals provided milk, meat, skins and blood. The blood was sometimes drunk mixed with milk or made into a kind of black pudding. Milk was used to make cheese and butter.
3. The farmers grew wheat for bread and porridge and barley for beer.
4. The Celts made mead from honey and they imported large amounts of wine from Europe.
5. Hunters killed wild pigs and deer.
6. The rivers provided fish and there were plenty of wild vegetables.

H. Buildings

1. The Irish Celts seem to have built their dwellings in exactly the same way as their Bronze Age predecessors.
2. They were very warlike and their more important rulers built large hillforts.
3. For a long time archaeologists thought that these were built only in Europe but aerial photographs show that a major hillfort was built at Brusselstown Hill, Co. Wicklow.
4. The Hill of Tara may have been one also but many archaeologists believe that it was a religious centre, not a military or political one.

I. Warfare

1. The Irish Celts loved fighting.
2. At every feast, each warrior's place at table was fixed according to his exploits.
3. Fights often occurred between warriors when they couldn't agree who was the more important.
4. A warrior's status depended on how many cattle he rustled and on how many enemies he beheaded.
5. The Celts believed that a man's spirit lived in his head and capturing a head brought good luck and added to a man's bravery.
6. Cattle-raiding, head-hunting and quarrels over status often led to battles.
7. The warriors rode to battle in their chariots – but rarely used them in the fighting.
8. At the beginning of a battle the chief warriors on each side boasted of their great deeds and challenged one another to single combat.
9. Indeed, most battles seem to have been a series of such individual fights.

10. At the end of the day, the army with the greater number of victims was declared the winner and the soldiers went home.
11. Sometimes, there were larger battles with all the warriors – and their wives – joining in.
12. Celtic warriors were armed with long slashing swords and short daggers for stabbing. They used throwing spears and some carried rectangular wooden shields.
13. However, they hardly ever wore armour and many warriors preferred to fight totally naked.
14. The Celts did not organise their armies very well and smaller, better-disciplined forces like the Roman army defeated them easily.

J. Religion
1. We know little about Celtic religion for they wrote down nothing about their beliefs.
2. However, it seems that the Celts believed in many gods. A lot of them were trinities (the Celts regarded the number three as being very important).
3. Dagda or the good god was their main god. There were others like Mannanaun, god of the sea, and Brigid, goddess of spring and lambs.
4. The Celts did not build temples. They did not believe that their gods could be confined in buildings.
5. Instead, they worshipped them in the open, often in sacred oak groves or at some sacred spring.
6. Druids (priests) offered prayers and sacrificed animal and human victims to their gods.

K. Art
1. The Celts built no great buildings or cities and no paintings have ever been discovered.
2. However, they decorated leather, metal and stone with complicated geometrical patterns and imaginary creatures.
3. This is called La Tène art, after a site in Switzerland where artifacts with similar decorations were discovered.
4. There are many stone carvings from Celtic times. Some are ogham stones, i.e. rough pillars with a name hammered into them.
5. Others are figures of people or gods – with the heads greatly emphasised.
6. There are also stones with abstract La Tène-type carvings, e.g. the Thuroe stone.

A silver bowl associated with the Celts in France.
Note the emphasis on the human head on the exterior panels.
Internally, infantry, cavalry and trumpeters are visible

NOTE: YOU MUST STUDY *EITHER* 3A, 3B OR 3C.

3A ANCIENT EGYPT

LAND AND PEOPLE

A. *The River Nile*
1. The Nile flows northwards for 6,500 km from Ethiopia to the Mediterranean. Its last 1,000 km are in Egypt.
2. Here the river cuts a narrow valley through the desert and just before flowing into the sea, it splits into many branches which criss-cross its delta.
3. Every July the Nile floods and deposits vast amounts of fertile soil on its valley floor.
4. The people of ancient Egypt built dams and ditches to control these floods and during the dry season they used a crane-like machine called a shaduf to lift water from the river to irrigate the land.

B. *The People*
1. The Egyptians were small and dark.
2. The men wore loincloths while the women wore long sleeveless dresses. They used types of head-dress to protect themselves from the sun and ointments to prevent blistering and sunburn. All Egyptians were very fond of ornaments and the very rich wore elaborate brooches, necklaces and rings of gold set with precious stones.
3. The fertile soils produced wheat, barley, flax, grapes, fruit and vegetables.
4. The Nile provided abundant fish for all but only the wealthy ate meat.
5. The poorer people drank beer, the richer drank wine.

C. *Houses*
1. The ordinary people lived in small huts made of sun-dried mud bricks. Windows were small and set high to keep out the heat but to let in some light.
2. Each hut contained a living-room and bedroom.
3. However, because the climate was warm and dry, people lived mostly in the yard at the back of the house. Here the food was cooked on a charcoal fire and bread was baked in an oven.
4. Steps led to the flat roof of the house. The people ate their meals and slept there during the hot time of year.
5. The rich lived in larger villas near the river. These villas had walled gardens and pools of water to keep the air cool.
6. The rooms of the villa were built around a central courtyard which acted as a living and dining area.

7. The poor had very little furniture. The rich had beds (with wooden neck-rests instead of pillows), low tables and chairs. The Egyptians had no cupboards and stored their food and goods in wooden chests or baskets.

THE OLD KINGDOM

A. Unification

1. At first Egypt contained two separate kingdoms, Upper Egypt in the valley and Lower Egypt in the delta.
2. About 3300 BC, Menes, king of Upper Egypt, conquered the delta and began the custom whereby the ruler of Egypt wore a double crown, the high white one of Upper Egypt and the flat red one of Lower Egypt.

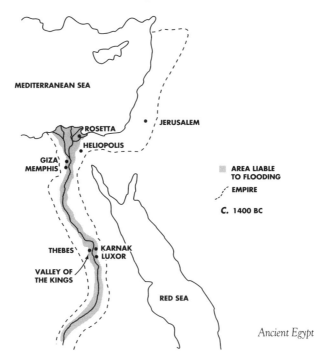

Ancient Egypt

B. The Pharaohs

1. Egypt's rulers were called pharaohs.
2. They were the country's chief priests, war leaders and law givers.
3. Most Egyptians believed that the pharaoh was a god and that after his death he would join the gods in the next world and continue to look after his country.
4. People treated the pharaoh with great respect.

C. The Pyramids

1. Dead pharaohs were buried in magnificent tombs with food, treasures and weapons for their use in the afterlife.
2. Many pharaohs from the Old Kingdom were buried in pyramids built near Giza.
3. The Step Pyramid, built for Pharaoh Djoser (c. 3000 BC), was the first.
4. Cheops' pyramid (c. 2600 BC) was the greatest. It is 225 metres square and 250 metres high. It contains two and a half million blocks of stone. The lightest weighs two and a half tonnes.
5. It is said that 100,000 workers spent twenty years building this great pyramid. Many were skilled masons and stone-cutters but the heavy labour of moving the great stones was carried out by the farmers during slack times in the agricultural year.
6. Somewhere in each pyramid was a small chamber for the pharaoh's mummified body. Its exact location was kept secret but nevertheless all the pyramids were eventually robbed.

D. Egypt's Gods

1. The Egyptians worshipped many gods. Ra, the sun god, was the most important. The Egyptians believed that he travelled across the sky each day in a boat, rowed by the spirits of the dead pharaohs.
2. Osiris was the god of the harvest and of eternal life. His wife, Isis, ruled the underworld.
3. The Egyptians believed that Osiris weighed each soul in a scales. If a person had led a good life and was able to recite certain magic spells, the scales balanced and Osiris granted the person eternal life.
4. These spells were obviously important. They were contained in *The Book of the Dead* and were often painted on tomb walls.

E. Mummies

1. The Egyptians embalmed the bodies of the dead by removing the intestines and by drying them out in a chemical called natron.
2. The bodies were then treated with ointments, wrapped in linen bandages, put in wooden or stone coffins and placed in a rectangular stone box called a sarcophagus.
3. The bodies of the poor were buried in the sand or in a cave.

THE NEW KINGDOM

A. Disintegration

1. Civil war raged in Egypt between 2300 and 2100 BC.
2. The Middle Kingdom began about 2100 BC when a new line of pharaohs took control.

3. In 1750 BC foreigners called Hykos, equipped with chariots and bronze weapons, overwhelmed the Egyptians and ruled the country for about one hundred and fifty years.

4. Then in 1600 BC Prince Amosis drove the Hykos from Egypt, beginning the era known as the New Kingdom.

B. Conquest

1. The pharaohs of the New Kingdom conquered the Sudan, Palestine and Syria and they marked the borders of their new empire with great pillars called obelisks.

2. Their greatest conquerors included Rameses II and Thothmes III.

3. They also included Queen Hatshepsut who sent a great trading expedition down the Red Sea to East Africa.

C. Temples

1. Heliopolis was the capital of the Old Kingdom. Thebes was the capital of the New Kingdom.

2. Its god, Amen, became very important in Egyptian religion and his name was linked with that of the sun god Ra. The two became united as Amen-Ra.

3. Many temples were built to honour him. These were massive structures, built mainly by slaves captured in battle. The most famous temple is that at Karnak, erected by Rameses II.

D. Egyptian Writing

1. The temples were warehouses, administrative centres, treasuries and schools as well as places of worship.

2. Their schools trained boys to become scribes.

3. Scribes kept records of the temples' property. They wrote down spells, legends, laws and medical prescriptions on papyrus, paper made from reeds.

4. The dry climate of Egypt has preserved many of these papyri thus helping us to build up a vivid picture of Egyptian life.

5. Egyptian scribes used three kinds of writing: hieroglyphic (sacred), hieratic (priestly) and demotic (ordinary).

6. Hieroglyphic writing was elaborate and slow to do and is found mainly on monuments. The other kinds are easier to write and occur mainly on papyri.

7. Egyptian writing fell out of use about AD 400 and people soon forgot how to read it.

8. The Rosetta Stone, discovered in 1799, contained inscriptions in hieroglyphic, demotic and Greek.

9. A French scholar, Jean François Champollion, guessed that the three inscriptions meant the same thing and he used the Greek text to decipher the Egyptian.

E. One God

1. The priests of Amen-Ra gradually became very powerful and eventually controlled up to one-third of the land of Egypt.
2. Amenhotep IV became pharaoh in 1370 BC.
3. He tried to destroy the priests' power by closing down their temples and by introducing the worship of a single god, Aton.
4. However, Amenhotep died before completing his task and the priests forced his son, Tutankhamun, to restore the old religion.

F. Tutankhamun's Tomb

1. Tutankhamun died when he was eighteen years old and he was buried in a tomb in the Valley of the Kings (1352 BC).
2. In 1922 Howard Carter discovered his burial place.
3. The tomb was filled with gold, jewels, weapons, chariots, furniture and ornaments. The mummy of the pharaoh was intact, encased in solidified perfume and covered with a magnificent golden mask.
4. Carter's discovery was the greatest find from the ancient world and a rich source of information about ancient Egypt.

*The superb workmanship of the ancient Egyptians can
be seen in this magnificent funerary mask
of Tutankhamun*

G. Decline and Fall

1. Gradually, Egyptian power declined.
2. There were civil wars between the priests and the pharaohs and between different pretenders to the throne.
3. Egypt had no iron and its armies were unable to resist foreign invaders equipped with iron weapons.
4. In 30 BC, Cleopatra, the last independent Egyptian ruler, killed herself and Egypt became a Roman province.

LEGACY

Although ancient Egypt is very remote in time and distance, it nevertheless left an important legacy to the modern world.

1. Egyptians developed paper and ink, materials on which much of our civilisation is built.
2. Egyptians developed some basic geometric ideas to deal with land surveying, so important in a country subject to flooding.
3. They evolved a calendar with a year 365 days long.
4. They were also very good surgeons. Their funeral practices gave them a good knowledge of anatomy. They set bones, extracted teeth and had a range of poultices to deal with cuts. However, they were not very good physicians and often relied on spells and magic potions to deal with non-surgical problems.

3B ANCIENT GREECE

MINOANS AND MYCENAEANS

A. The Minoans of Crete

1. The Minoan civilisation (named after King Minos) flourished on Crete *c.* 2000 BC.
2. The Minoans grew cereals, vines and olives and made fine pottery and jewellery.
3. They built great fleets, traded their surplus produce throughout the eastern Mediterranean, and for a time dominated the region.
4. The Minoans were small, with copper-coloured skin and long dark hair.
5. The men wore striped loincloths or baggy trousers. The women wore long, flounced skirts and short-sleeved jackets. They seem to have admired thin waists and wore tight belts to show them off.

6.   The Minoans did not build great temples but worshipped an earth-goddess in mountain and woodland shrines. The double-axe or labrys seems to have been her symbol. They also made statues of a snake-goddess to protect the homes of the people.

B. Knossos

1.   The rulers of Crete built many great palaces. The most important, at Knossos, was excavated by Sir Arthur Evans in the 1900s.
2.   Evans found a maze of passages, store-rooms and royal apartments grouped around a great courtyard. There was a throne-room and a bathroom plumbed for running water.
3.   The walls were decorated with bright pictures of birds, plants, sea-creatures and of contestants taking part in bull-jumping.
4.   Evans also found clay tablets with two types of writing, Linear A and Linear B. Linear A has not yet been deciphered. Michael Ventris discovered that Linear B was an early type of Greek. The tablets contain the palace accounts.

C. The Mycenaeans

1.   The Minoan civilisation was overwhelmed about 1500 BC, probably by Mycenaean peoples from mainland Greece.
2.   The Mycenaean chiefs lived in massive stone fortresses, e.g. Mycenae and Pylos, and they seem to have been more interested in piracy and war than in trade.
3.   Many bronze weapons have been found from this time and their Linear B tablets contain long lists of military equipment.
4.   The story of Troy was probably based on one of their piratical raids.

D. The Dark Ages

1.   All the Mycenaean fortresses were destroyed about 1250 BC, probably by invaders armed with iron weapons.
2.   Greece now entered a Dark Age during which people forgot how to write, how to paint fresco, how to make good pottery or how to create other works of art.
3.   The Dark Ages came to an end about 750 BC with the creation of the city-states and the civilisation associated with classical Greece.

THE EMERGENCE OF CLASSICAL GREECE

A. The People

1.   The Greeks called themselves Hellenes and their country Hellas.
2.   They belonged to the same race, spoke the same language, worshipped the same gods and lived in small self-governing communities called city-states.
3.   However, they frequently quarrelled with one another, though at the same time regarding all outsiders as 'barberoi' (savages).

4. Greek styles changed little. Men wore a short tunic and draped themselves in a cloak called a himation. Women wore a long woollen dress called a peplos or a lighter one called a chiton.

B. The City-States

1. Each city-state or polis was small, mostly self-contained, and isolated from its neighbours by mountains and the sea.
2. A polis usually controlled enough farmland to feed its citizens but if the population became too large its surplus people emigrated to found a colony somewhere else in the Mediterranean. The classical Greek world included territory which does not belong to modern Greece.
3. The centre of each polis was usually an acropolis, i.e. a fortress-temple-palace built on a hill.
4. The ordinary people lived in tiny mud-bricked houses but all important public events took place in the agora (market-place), which was usually surrounded by colonnaded arcades.

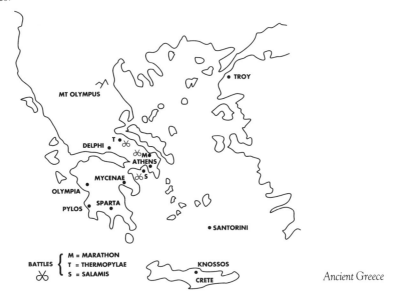

Ancient Greece

C. Greek Religion

1. The Greeks took many of their religious ideas from the Minoans, Mycenaeans and Egyptians.
2. They also changed their religious ideas from time to time.
3. However, they believed in many gods who controlled all aspects of life and who had to be kept happy with prayers, ceremonies and sacrifices.
4. The most important gods, called the Pantheon, lived on Mount Olympus. Zeus was father of the gods. Poseidon ruled the sea. Athena was goddess of wisdom. Ares was god of war. Aphrodite was goddess of love and beauty.

5. Each city and activity had its own god and success or failure depended on the good or bad will of the gods.
6. To discover the wishes of the gods, the Greeks consulted the priestess called The Oracle at Delphi. However, she often spoke in riddles and was frequently misunderstood.

D. The Olympic Games

1. The Greeks held many festivals to honour the gods. The most famous was the Olympic games.
2. These were held every four years between 776 BC and AD 393 at Olympia.
3. All fighting had to stop during the Olympics. Contestants from all over the Greek world took part. The victors were rewarded with olive wreaths and were treated as heroes by their cities.
4. Important events included (i) the Stade, a sprint; (ii) the Hoplitodrome, a race run wearing armour; (iii) the Pentathlon; (iv) the Pancration, a form of combat; and (v) chariot-racing.

E. The Persian Wars

1. Many Greek colonies were located in Asia Minor, a region which was part of the Persian empire.
2. The Greeks rebelled. They were easily defeated and Darius, the Persian emperor, decided to add Greece itself to his empire.
3. In 490 BC a Persian army invaded Greece but was defeated at Marathon.
4. In 480 BC Emperor Xerxes invaded Greece again. He defeated a Spartan army at Thermopylae. He captured and burned Athens but was defeated at the great naval battle of Salamis.
5. The Greeks owed their land victories to their hoplites. These soldiers were equipped with helmets, chest armour, shields and spears, and fought in massed formation to the sound of fife and drum.
6. They owed their naval victories to their triremes, fast ships powered by three banks of oars and equipped with a ram to sink enemy ships.
7. Following their victory over the Persians, the Greeks enjoyed a 'Golden Age' of peace and prosperity.
8. During this time two city-states, Athens and Sparta, dominated Greece.

ATHENS

A. Democracy
1. Athens was a democracy. It was ruled by its citizens, i.e. all adult males. Women, foreigners and slaves were not citizens.
2. The citizens met in Assembly on the Pnyx to make laws, to elect the army's ten generals and the many officials needed to run the city.
3. A Council of 501 was chosen by lot to carry out the decisions of the Assembly and to try criminals. Nobody could be a member of the Council for more than two years and so every citizen had a good chance of taking part in government.
4. Any citizen who seemed to be too powerful could be ostracised (sent into exile) by a vote of the Assembly.

B. Education
1. The Athenians believed that boys should learn to become good citizens.
2. Some boys were taught at home by tutors. Others attended schools run by pedagogues.
3. They learned about the heroes and the gods by reading the poems of Homer from papyrus rolls. They learned to write with a stylus on wax-covered boards. They also learned music and took part in athletic events to make them fit to serve in the army.
4. At fifteen, the sons of the poor went to learn a trade. The sons of the rich continued their education under sophists (wise men) and learned rhetoric (public speaking) so that they could take part in politics.

C. Women in Athens
1. Women were not citizens and received very little education.
2. Mothers taught their daughters sewing and weaving but slaves did the heavy work like cleaning and cooking.
3. Women spent most of their time at home and rarely appeared in public.
4. They married at fourteen or fifteen and could not own any property.

D. The City
1. A general called Pericles was one of the most influential men in Athens.
2. He persuaded the people to build defensive walls around the city and to construct the Long Walls linking it with the port of Piraeus so that supplies could be obtained even in wartime.
3. He was mainly responsible for building the Parthenon and the other temples on the Acropolis.
4. The houses of the ordinary people were small, flimsy mud-brick buildings. Rooms were small and opened onto a courtyard. The women were usually confined to the upper floors.

A model of the Acropolis. Note the Parthenon (the main temple) and the statue of Athena in the centre

5. Streets were narrow, twisting and unpaved. There were no gutters or drains and therefore there was a great contrast between the glorious public buildings and the slums inhabited by the people.

SPARTA

A. Military State
1. Sparta was ruled by a military aristocracy.
2. The soldiers' Assembly elected two kings to command the army and to lead the worship of the gods. They chose five overseers to manage public affairs and a Council of Elders to advise the Assembly.
3. The Spartans were not interested in agriculture, trade or industry. Most of this work was carried out by helots (slaves). The Spartans treated the helots very badly and sometimes massacred groups of them to frighten the others.

B. Military Training
1. The Spartans were interested only in war.
2. Mothers were told to exercise so that their children would be healthy. Unhealthy babies were exposed to die.
3. At seven, a Spartan boy went to live in an army barracks. He was beaten regularly, given few clothes and encouraged to steal food.

4. At twelve, he began weapons training and to become a citizen he had to live apart from the community for a period, living by his wits – and killing helots.

5. Not surprisingly, the Spartans made brave, disciplined, ruthless soldiers – and won many prizes at the Olympic games.

6. A Spartan married at twenty but he continued to live in barracks until he was sixty.

C. Spartan Women

1. Spartan women had more freedom than other Greek women.

2. They were better educated. They took part in athletic competitions and because their husbands were often away at war, they had to take control of their households and helots.

3. They were also expected to encourage their menfolk to return from battle 'with their shields or on them', i.e. having fought honourably or died.

GREEK CULTURE

A. Drama

1. Drama was first used in religious ceremonies and the earliest plays were about the gods and heroes.

2. The actors used high-heeled shoes, padded robes and masks to make them appear superhuman. The mouths of the masks were shaped to amplify the actors' voices.

3. Aeschylus, 'the father of tragedy', wrote plays about gods and heroes.

4. Aristophanes wrote comedies poking fun at self-important people.

B. The Theatres

1. Greek theatres were open to the air.

2. The seats were arranged in semicircles around the orchestra where the action took place.

3. The proscenium (stage) stood behind the orchestra and the skene (dressing-rooms) was further back.

4. Greek theatres were very large. The theatre at Epidaurus could hold 17,000 spectators.

5. They were also renowned for the quality of their sound. Even the slightest whisper from the orchestra could be heard throughout the building.

C. Philosophy

1. Athens was famous for its many philosophers (people who loved wisdom).

2. Socrates, 'the father of philosophy', tried to find out the truth about things by continually asking questions. Many felt that his questioning would anger the gods. He was found guilty of showing them disrespect and was forced to kill himself.

The theatre at Epidaurus. The ruins on the right are the remains of the skene

3. Plato was a follower of Socrates. He had a school called the Academy and wrote down many of Socrates' ideas. In his book *The Republic* he declared that a wise and good king was better for a city than democracy.

4. Aristotle was interested in everything. He wrote about psychology, philosophy, astronomy, geography, literature, art . . . He greatly influenced the scholars of the Middle Ages. They believed that he was always correct though, in fact, he was often wrong about scientific matters.

D. Science

There were many famous scientists in ancient Greece.

1. Archimedes explained the law of the lever and discovered that floating bodies displace their own weight in water.

2. Pythagoras declared that the world was round and Eratosthenes measured its circumference.

3. Euclid discovered the fundamental rules of geometry.

4. Hippocrates, 'the father of medicine', refused to believe that evil spirits caused disease. He developed cures for some diseases and laid down the basic rules of behaviour for doctors.

ALEXANDER THE GREAT

1. In 338 BC Philip of Macedonia and his son Alexander conquered all Greece.
2. Alexander was only twenty when he became ruler of Macedonia in 336 BC. However, he was one of the world's greatest generals and before he died in 323 BC he had conquered the enormous Persian empire.
3. He founded many cities and his soldiers who settled in them brought the Greek language and Greek culture to much of the Middle East.
4. Alexandria, in Egypt, was the most important of these cities and it became the greatest centre of learning in the ancient world.
5. Alexander had a great appetite for knowledge. Aristotle was one of his tutors and he brought many scholars on his expeditions.
6. He wished all the people of his empire to live peacefully together. However, his Greek and Macedonian soldiers refused to treat the Persians as equals. His generals quarrelled with one another and when he died his empire broke up. Its fragments were later conquered by the Romans.

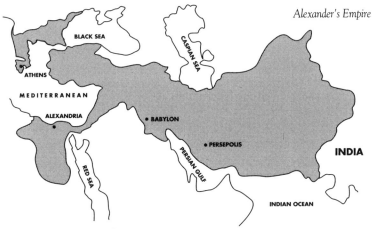

Alexander's Empire

WHAT WE OWE THE GREEKS

1. The alphabet is derived from the Greek system of writing and many Greek words are used in the languages of Europe.
2. Most of our political ideas originated in Greece.
3. Our ideas of poetry, drama, architecture and sculpture come directly from the ancient Greeks.
4. Most of our basic scientific and mathematical knowledge was discovered in ancient Greece.
5. Although Christianity originated among the Jews of Palestine, a province of the Roman empire, the Christian Scriptures were written in Greek and first reached Europe through Greece.

THE RISE AND FALL OF ROME

A. Foundation
1. According to legend, Romulus founded Rome in 753 BC.
2. Archaeology shows that a village was founded on the site of Rome about this date.
3. Etruscan kings ruled Rome until 509 BC when the Romans expelled the last, Tarquin the Proud, and set up a republic, i.e. a state controlled by the people.

B. Growth
1. The new republic had to fight many enemies to survive but by 265 BC the Romans controlled most of Italy.
2. They now came into conflict with Carthage, a powerful naval and trading city in North Africa.
3. Rome won the three Punic Wars which followed. Carthage and its allies were destroyed and by 146 BC Rome was master of most of the Mediterranean basin.

C. Civil War
1. Rome's generals had built up huge armies during these wars. Now they fought one another to control the state.
2. These wars ended in 31 BC when Augustus, Rome's first emperor, defeated Antony at Actium.

Soldiers of the Praetorian guard, the emperor's own bodyguards

D. *Pax Romana*
1. For two centuries the empire experienced the Pax Romana, peace and prosperity preserved by well-defended natural frontiers, a great army, an efficient administration and good emperors such as Augustus and Trajan.
2. At this time Christianity became established in the empire.

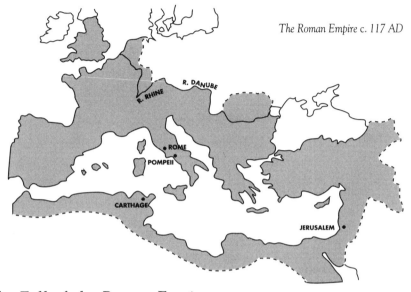

The Roman Empire c. 117 AD

E. *The Fall of the Roman Empire*
The empire began to break up about AD 300.
1. It had became too costly and too complicated to administer properly.
2. People were unhappy with high taxes.
3. Various generals used this unhappiness as an excuse to try to take over the empire.
4. The civil wars that followed greatly weakened the empire and it was finally shattered by waves of barbarians who entered Europe from Asia in the fourth and fifth centuries.
5. Romulus Augustulus, the last emperor of Rome, was overthrown in AD 476.

THE LEGACY OF ROME

Although the Roman empire broke up 1,500 years ago, it still influences us in many ways.
1. Many of Europe's languages, e.g. French and Spanish, evolved from Latin, the language of the Romans.
2. Most other European languages have loan words and grammatical constructions taken from Latin.
3. Christianity spread into Europe from Rome and the pope, the bishop of Rome, is head of the world's largest Christian community.

4. Most European laws are based on laws enacted by Napoleon Bonaparte in the 1800s. These, in turn, were based mainly on the laws of ancient Rome.
5. Nowadays, most Europeans live in towns and cities. (i) Many of these were founded by the Romans. (ii) The Romans often designed their cities according to a grid-iron pattern. This pattern is still followed in many parts of the world.
6. The Romans left numerous fine works of art for us to enjoy.
7. These works of art are still used as models and standards by many artists.

HOW THE ROMANS LIVED

A. Sources
We know a great deal about Roman life.
1. The ruins of many Roman buildings, e.g. at Pompeii, enable us to reconstruct them as they were.
2. Statues and frescoes show us how the Romans looked and dressed.
3. Their prolific writings tell us how they worked, what they ate and how they enjoyed themselves.

B. The City of Rome
1. Rome was the centre of the empire.
2. With over one million inhabitants, Rome was the largest city of the ancient world.
3. Ships sailed into Ostia (Rome's port) bringing grain from North Africa, wool from Britain, wine from France, copper from Spain, silk from China, and spices from the Orient.
4. (i) Eleven aqueducts brought water to Rome from the eastern hills. (ii) The water was stored in giant cisterns and then distributed through lead pipes to over a thousand fountains from which the ordinary people took what they needed. (iii) Some rich people had water piped directly into their houses.
5. (i) Space was very scarce in imperial Rome and most people had to live in large blocks of flats called insulae. (ii) There were about fifty thousand such insulae but fewer than two thousand private houses. (iii) The insulae were six or seven storeys high. The lower storeys were stone-built and were occupied by the wealthy. (iv) The upper storeys were timber-built and were occupied by poorer people. (v) Shops usually occupied the ground floors.
6. (i) In winter the insulae were heated by charcoal burning in bronze basins. (ii) Outbreaks of fire were frequent and spread easily from building to building across the narrow, twisting streets and lanes. (iii) No wonder Rome needed a permanent fire brigade of 7,000 men.

C. Starting the Day

1. (i) Romans got out of bed early. (ii) They had little for breakfast – crusts, fruit and a little well-watered wine.
2. At home Romans wore knee-length tunics, but when they left their insulae they put on their togas. These were huge rectangles of woollen cloth, heavy and awkward but considered dignified.
3. Before going to work, the men called on their patrons, people who belonged to a higher social class whom they supported and who paid them a small cash allowance.
4. (i) A person's status depended on his patron's position in society and on the number and status of his own clients. (ii) In Rome, almost everyone was at once a patron and a client.

D. Workers and Slaves

1. Many Romans were craftsmen, traders or civil servants.
2. Many were unemployed and depended on free grain from the government.
3. Slaves did all the hard work around the city. (i) Many slaves had been captured in war and others had been born into slave families. (ii) Slaves had no legal rights, e.g. their masters could have them executed at will. (iii) However, most masters treated their slaves well and those with special skills, e.g. doctors, scribes or teachers, could earn enough money to buy their freedom. (iv) Because slaves had none of the rights of Roman citizens and could never take control of the state, emperors often used them for important government work.

E. Women

1. Roman women took no part in public life.
2. Most girls married at fourteen or fifteen.
3. The wives of poor men stayed at home and did housework.
4. The wives of richer men supervised their slaves, visited friends or received visitors.
5. Women wore an ankle-length dress and a stola (cloak).
6. They took great care of their appearance, paying special attention to their hair.
7. Many wore wigs made from human hair imported from India.
8. Hair fashion changed quickly and sculptors made detachable stone wigs so that the portrait busts of their clients would always be in fashion.

F. School

1. Boys and girls alike attended school.
2. There were no state-run schools and anybody could open one.
3. Classes were usually held in the open, often near a forum (market-place).
4. Pupils learned to write with a stylus on wax-covered boards and they learned to read from papyrus manuscripts. These manuscripts were dictated letter by letter and written down by groups of scribes working in manuscript factories.

5. Students were easily distracted by their surroundings and were flogged severely whenever their attention strayed or when they did not know their homework.

G. Holidays

1. The schoolchildren had every eighth day free. This was the market day when every forum in the city was busy with people buying and selling.
2. Another important holiday was the Saturnalia celebrated in late December. (i) People gave one another presents in honour of the god Saturn. (ii) Children were allowed to break the rules their parents normally enforced. (iii) Masters often served their slaves at table. (iv) Many of these customs became part of the Christmas celebrations.

H. The Baths

1. Most Romans stopped work early in the afternoon and after a light lunch they visited the public baths.
2. There were over a thousand in Rome.
3. Most were quite small. They were privately owned and their owners made a living by charging admission fees.
4. There were several large baths built by the emperors. The baths of Caracalla covered over thirty acres and could accommodate 35,000 customers.
5. All baths were designed according to the same principles. (i) The customers left their clothes in a waiting-room and (ii) swam in a warm pool called the tepidarium. (iii) Then they moved into the calidarium which was superheated like a sauna. (iv) Finally, they swam in a cold pool called the frigidarium.
6. The Romans had no soap and they cleaned themselves by rubbing oil on their skins and scraping it off with a strigil (scraper).
7. Most baths had gymnasia and some had libraries and theatres.

I. The Evening

1. After bathing, the Romans went home for the evening meal.
2. This usually consisted of cold meat, fish, vegetables, bread and wine.
3. Some wealthy Romans held lavish feasts for their friends.
4. The Romans generally went to bed when darkness fell.
5. Artificial light was expensive and not very effective.

J. Chariot-Racing

1. On public holidays Romans enjoyed chariot-racing and fighting.
2. Chariot-racing took place at the Circus Maximus, a huge arena able to hold up to 250,000 spectators.
3. Charioteers belonged to one of four teams – Greens, Blues, Reds and Whites.

4. Two chariots from each team took part in each race. One of the charioteers tried to block the other teams while his companion went on to win.

5. Chariots were light and four horses pulled them around the course at great speed. This, and the blocking tactics they employed, caused many deaths.

6. Each team had its fanatical supporters who placed heavy bets on their favourite charioteers – and frequently fought pitched battles with their rivals.

K. The Arena

1. In amphitheatres such as the Colosseum, gladiators entertained the crowds by killing one another or by slaughtering animals.

2. Some gladiators were criminals, others were prisoners of war, others fought because they liked the life.

3. Gladiators trained in special schools and used special weapons such as a curved sword and small shield or net and trident.

4. Sometimes, a gladiator on the point of killing an enemy would appeal to a crowd for mercy. If they were pleased, the spectators held up their thumbs. If they were not, they turned them down, indicating that the gladiator should plunge his sword into his defeated enemy.

5. Sometimes, gladiators who had won many battles were given a wooden sword as a token of freedom. Many rejected it, preferring the thrills, fame and money of the amphitheatre.

L. Pompeii: A Provincial Town

1. Pompeii was a small town situated on the bay of Naples.

2. On 24 August AD 79 the nearby Mount Vesuvius exploded.

3. Within minutes, thousands had choked on the volcano's poisonous fumes.

4. Within hours, the city was buried by volcanic debris.

5. Centuries passed before it was rediscovered.

6. Systematic excavations by Giuseppe Fiorelli exposed streets, villas, workshops and public buildings.

7. He found that Pompeii consisted of rectangular blocks of buildings with the streets meeting at right angles. The streets were narrow but paved and stepping-stones led from footpath to footpath. Pedestrians could therefore cross the streets without stepping into dirt and mud. These stepping-stones also acted like modern ramps in slowing down the traffic.

8. Many people lived in villas rather than in insulae.

9. The rooms were arranged around a central yard and gardens.

10. Many villa-owners let out parts of their villas as shops.

11. One such shop served fast food from large pots set into the counters. These pots contained oil, wine and snacks.

The forum (market place) of Pompeii. Mount Vesuvius is visible in the background

12. The people of Pompeii enjoyed a rich social life. There were several large public baths, two theatres and an amphitheatre in the town.

13. Archaeologists have discovered many graffiti. (i) Some urged the readers to vote for particular candidates in local elections. (ii) Others announced public meetings or sales or (iii) offered rewards for goods recovered. (iv) More abused particular individuals.

14. During his excavations, (i) Fiorelli discovered many hollows in the soft muddy rocks and ashes. (ii) He filled these with plaster and when it hardened he found that they were models of people killed during the eruption. (iii) These models included prisoners locked in jail, the guard at the town gate, a woman and her daughters killed trying to escape, priests from the temple of Isis killed at dinner, a chained dog . . .

M. The Dead

1. Few Romans ended their lives as spectacularly as the gladiators or the people of Pompeii.

2. Most died from illness or old age.

3. The Romans usually burned their dead and placed their ashes in tombs that lined the highways.

4. They often offered wine or food to the spirits of the dead to sustain them in the afterlife.

5. Christians, who began to settle in Rome about this time, did not follow this custom.

6. Instead, they buried their dead in underground passages called catacombs.

4 EARLY CHRISTIAN IRELAND

THE CONVERSION OF IRELAND

A. The First Christians
1. In 431 Pope Celestine sent Bishop Paladius to the 'Irish who believed in Christ'.
2. We hear nothing more about Paladius but it is obvious that there were Christians in Ireland at the time – i.e. before St Patrick is supposed to have begun his mission in 432.
3. We know little about these Christians. Perhaps they were slaves or traders from Europe or Irish people who had been converted by unknown missionaries from Europe.

B. St Patrick
1. Patrick was born in northern Britain, the son of a Roman official.
2. He was captured by pirates, and herded animals, possibly on Slemish in Co. Antrim.
3. He escaped to Europe but returned to Ireland as a missionary bishop in 432.
4. Patrick wrote an autobiography, the *Confessio*, and his letter to King Coroticus also survives.
5. Patrick spent most of his time in the northern half of the country, with his headquarters in Armagh.
6. He usually tried to convert kings and nobles, believing that the ordinary people would follow their masters' example.
7. While Patrick was working in the north, other missionaries were active in the south, e.g. Auxilius and Secundinus.
8. When Patrick died in 461, there were many Christians in Ireland.
9. However, many pagan customs still lived on. For example, springs sacred to pagan gods became associated with Christian saints, and Brehon laws which allowed polygamy and divorce remained in force for many centuries.

THE IRISH MONASTERIES

A. The First Monasteries
1. St Enda set up Ireland's first monastery on the Aran Islands in 490.
2. During the following centuries many more monasteries were established.
3. Some were in well-populated areas where the monks were able to help the poor and the sick.
4. Others were in remote places where nobody would disturb the monks at their prayers and contemplation.

B. What the Monasteries Looked Like

1. An early Irish monastery looked like a large ringfort.
2. The monks lived in circular wattle-and-daub huts built within an earthen bank or stone caiseal.
3. There were also larger, barn-like buildings where the monks met for mass, prayer and worship.

A reconstruction of the monastery at Kells. Note the circular enclosure, the beehive huts, the tiny churches and the round tower

4. Most of these structures were timber-built but in the west, where timber was scarce, the monks used stone.
5. The monks on Skellig Michael and Inishmurray made beehive huts using the corbelling method.
6. In other places, they built small rectangular churches with steep stone roofs, e.g. St Molua's Church in Killaloe.

C. Round Towers

1. Some monasteries, e.g. Glendalough and Ardmore, had round towers.
2. The Irish for round tower is 'clog teach' or bell-house.
3. They were also used as look-out points and store-houses.
4. However, they were bad refuges as a well-placed fire could turn them into fiery chimneys.
5. Round towers were twenty-five to thirty-five metres high. The door was about four metres above ground level and could be reached only by ladder. Internally the towers were divided into several storeys by wooden floors connected by ladder. Each storey had a window and the top storey usually had four or eight.

D. Life in the Monasteries

1. The monasteries were totally self-contained.
2. The monks grew their own food and caught fish in the rivers and sea.
3. They made their own clothes and whatever leather, timber or metal goods they required.
4. When the monks were not working or praying, they studied the Scriptures and the classics. Some monasteries such as Bangor or Glendalough have been compared to university cities.
5. The rules laid down for Irish monks were very strict.
6. They had to work hard, to say many prayers, to study, to eat little and to sleep little.
7. They had to obey the abbot in everything and those who broke the rule of the monastery were compelled to endure long fasts or severe floggings.

E. A Church Run by Abbots

1. Patrick and the early missionaries organised the Church in dioceses and parishes.
2. However, as there were no towns in Ireland where bishops could set up their headquarters, the monasteries became the centre of Christianity.
3. Thus abbots, rather than bishops, ruled the early Church in Ireland.

F. Manuscripts

1. There were no printed books until the sixteenth century and all books had to be copied by hand on vellum or parchment.
2. The oldest surviving Irish manuscript is a copy of the psalms.
3. This dates from c. 560 and is nicknamed the 'Cathach' because for centuries the O'Donnell family carried it into battle as a lucky charm.
4. The Cathach has very little decoration.
5. The monks also produced illuminated manuscripts. These are copies of the Gospels decorated with complicated, colourful abstract designs and homely sketches of farmyard animals and everyday life.
6. The Book of Durrow is the oldest surviving illuminated manuscript while the Book of Kells is the most famous.

G. Metalwork

1. The monasteries also produced important works of art in metal, e.g. the Ardagh Chalice and the shrine for St Patrick's bell.
2. These objects were made from silver or bronze with complicated patterns of gold thread, enamel and glass soldered onto them.
3. The designs are very similar to those in the illuminated manuscripts.

H. Crosses

1. Many monasteries had stone crosses, sometimes called high crosses, e.g. The Cross of Muiredeach at Monasterboice.
2. The earliest crosses were simple carvings on slabs of rock.
3. Later ones were more complex, with the shaft and arms divided into panels showing scenes from the Bible.
4. These panels were probably painted and may have been used to teach Scripture.
5. Typically, circles of stone joined the arms with the shaft.
6. Sometimes, the top of a cross was decorated with a stone model of a wooden church.

The Cross of Muiredeach, Monasterboice. Note the panels on the shaft showing biblical scenes and the stone model of a wooden church on the top

THE MISSIONARY MOVEMENT

A. Missionaries

Many Irish monks emigrated to work as missionaries in Europe.

B. St Colmcille (521–597)

1. Colmcille was a prince of Donegal.
2. He became a monk and founded monasteries at Durrow, Derry and Kells.
3. He made a copy of a friend's psalter (traditionally the Cathach) and refused to hand it over when he returned the original.

4. A battle followed at Culdreimna and there were many casualties.
5. In great distress Colmcille went into exile on Iona swearing never to set foot in Ireland again and promising to convert a pagan for every soul lost at Culdreimna.
6. Colmcille spent from 563 to 597 in Scotland and with his followers converted many of the native Picts to Christianity.
7. Iona became the centre of Scottish Christianity, culture and learning and also exercised great political influence.

C. *St Columbanus (543–615)*
1. In 590 Columbanus, abbot of Bangor, sailed to Europe with twelve companions.
2. They travelled through France, Switzerland and Germany converting the pagan peoples to Christianity.
3. They founded many monasteries, e.g. Luxeuil in France and St Gallen in Switzerland.
4. Columbanus was also famous as a great scholar and writer, and as an adviser to rulers and popes.
5. He died in his monastery at Bobbio while resting on a journey from Switzerland to Rome.

D. *Achievements*
1. Irish monks kept Christianity alive in many parts of Europe and revived it where it had died out.
2. They were also famous for their great knowledge of the Greek and Roman classics and they preserved and revived learning wherever they went.
3. They founded many monasteries. These often became the centres of town life, e.g. St Gallen in Switzerland and Würzburg in Germany.
4. However, the monks' successors quickly abandoned the very strict Irish monastic rule and used instead the gentler Benedictine Rule.

5   THE MIDDLE AGES

MEDIEVAL SOCIETY: THOSE WHO FOUGHT

A. *Society*
1. The Middle Ages lasted from *c.* AD 800 to *c.* 1400.
2. During this time European people were divided into three groups: (i) those who fought, (ii) those who prayed and (iii) those who laboured.

B. Feudalism

1. During the Middle Ages, rulers divided their lands among their great nobles.
2. These nobles divided their estates among lesser lords who then subdivided them among the knights.
3. The king alone owned the land.
4. Those who received land were called vassals.
5. Those who gave out land were known as lords.
6. The estates were called fiefs and lords lent them out to their vassals in return for (i) loyalty, (ii) military service, (iii) hospitality, (iv) advice and (v) money payments.
7. This social structure was called feudalism and the various groups formed the feudal pyramid.

C. The Ceremony of Infeudation

1. An elaborate ceremony took place when a man became a vassal.
2. Few people could read or write and a special ceremony was needed so that people would know exactly what lord and vassal had agreed.
3. During the ceremony the vassal (i) knelt, (ii) declared his loyalty to his lord and (iii) requested a fief.
4. The lord (i) promised to defend his vassal, (ii) raised him to his feet and (iii) gave him some symbol of his fief.

D. Training the Knight

1. At seven a boy began to train as a knight when he became a page.
2. He spent seven years learning the complicated etiquette of a nobleman.
3. At fourteen he became a squire. The squire learned (i) how to ride a horse in battle, (ii) how to take care of his master's weapons and armour and (iii) how to use them. (iv) He also accompanied his lord into battle.
4. When he was twenty-one the squire was dubbed a knight. (i) The squire spent the night before his investiture in prayer. (ii) Next morning he attended mass, during which his sword was placed on the altar as an offering to God. (iii) The senior knight present then tapped him on the shoulder with his sword thus making him a knight.
5. Sometimes a soldier 'won his spurs' on the battlefield when he was knighted for bravery.

E. Chivalry

1. Knights were supposed to follow a code of conduct called chivalry.
2. Chivalry demanded that knights (i) be brave, (ii) be polite to noblewomen, (iii) be kind to the poor, (iv) show devotion to the Church, and (v) be loyal to their lords.
3. However, very few knights lived up to the code of chivalry, especially in their dealings with the poor.

F. Castles

1. Castles were the homes of the knights and places of refuge in time of war.
2. Castles varied greatly in size and construction.
3. The Norman invaders of Ireland built temporary earth-and-timber fortifications called mottes and baileys. Some of these were later replaced by permanent stone structures, e.g. at Trim.
4. Such a castle (i) was protected by a moat with (ii) a drawbridge leading to a gate which could be closed by (iii) a portcullis. (iv) The castle walls had battlements from which the defenders could fire down on attackers. (v) If the walls were captured the defenders could retreat to the donjon or keep. This was a massive tower which also doubled as the castle-owner's living quarters.
5. If attackers failed to capture a castle in the first rush, they had to lay siege to it. If they had time and plenty of food, they could starve out the defenders.
6. (i) If they were in a hurry they could try to destroy the walls by digging mines underneath them. (ii) They could use battering-rams to knock them down and siege-towers and ladders to get soldiers over them. (iii) Catapults were also available to throw missiles into the castle.

A reconstruction of Trim Castle, the largest Norman fortress in Ireland. Note the central keep, the curtain walls, the moat and the well-protected barbican gateway on the right

G. The Knights in Battle

1. Knights formed the backbone of medieval armies.
2. They wore armour, helmets and shields for protection and they fought with lances, swords, hatchets and maces.
3. Most battles involved massed cavalry charges during which the knights stabbed and hacked one another until one side broke and ran away.

This section of the Bayeux tapestry shows soldiers wearing the chain mail armour of the early Middle Ages. Later, knights wore armour made from sheets of steel while helmets covering the entire face came into fashion

4.   Knights dominated battlefields until the fifteenth century. Then crossbows and longbows became powerful enough to fire arrows able to penetrate their armour.

5.   Guns able to destroy castle walls also became available.

6.   The knights were therefore no longer useful in war and their military importance came to an end.

MEDIEVAL SOCIETY: THOSE WHO PRAYED

A. The Clergy

1.   During the Middle Ages, most Europeans were Christians.
2.   The bishop of Rome, i.e. the pope, was head of the Church.
3.   A small group of clergymen called cardinals helped him.
4.   When a pope died, the cardinals elected his successor.
5.   Europe was divided into many dioceses. A bishop, picked by the local king or elected by the senior priests, ruled each diocese.
6.   Popes, cardinals and bishops were very important people and they seldom came in contact with the ordinary people.
7.   The parish clergy looked after the ordinary people.

B. The Parish Clergy

1.   The parish clergy came mainly from the ordinary people.
2.   They learned their profession directly from ordained priests.
3.   When they thought that they were ready for ordination, a bishop examined them orally and then ordained them.
4.   Few priests were well educated. Many were illiterate and were unable to teach their people very much about religion.
5.   As a result few medieval people knew much about their religion and superstition was widespread.

C.   The Importance of Religion

1.   Nevertheless, religion was central to most people's lives.
2.   The church was usually the best building in the village.
3.   Everyone met there for mass on Sunday and on the many feast-days of the period.
4.   All the major events of life – birth, marriage, death – were celebrated in the church.
5.   The church also served as a meeting hall and fairs and dances were often held in the church yard.
6.   The priest was given a tithe (one-tenth) of the value of the people's crops. This (i) paid his salary, (ii) kept the church in good repair and (iii) provided help for the needy.

Amiens Cathedral. Note the gothic features: pointed arches, complicated decoration and the numerous pillar-statues along the front of the building

D.   The Monks

1.   Many clergymen were monks.
2.   They lived in monasteries and followed the Rule of St Benedict, working, praying and studying.
3.   Most monasteries were built around a cloistered garden. The buildings included (i) a church, (ii) a refectory, (iii) a chapter house, (iv) dormitories, (v) a guest house, (vi) the abbot's house, (vii) a hospital, (viii) a library, (ix) workshops and (x) a scriptorium.
4.   The monks prayed in the church seven times daily.
5.   At other times, they slept, meditated and worked.

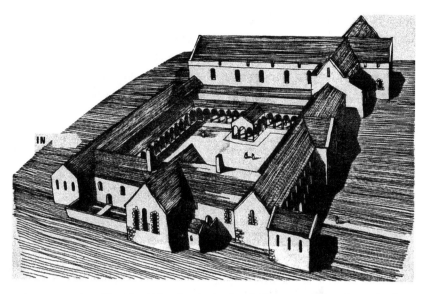

A reconstruction of Jerpoint Abbey showing its church, cloisters and the refectory (at the bottom of the picture). A tower was added later

6. Monasteries were the main centres of civilisation during the Dark Ages (c. AD 400–800). They preserved much of the learning of Greece and Rome. They were often the only places where the needy were helped and the young educated.
7. Noblemen frequently endowed monasteries.
8. Some monasteries became rich and standards of behaviour sometimes declined.
9. Attempts to reform them led to the creation of orders such as the Cistercians and Carthusians.

E. The Friars
1. Many people abandoned the Church during the thirteenth century.
2. Some could not believe Church doctrines.
3. Others fell away because of corrupt clergymen.
4. Neither the parish clergy nor the monks could deal with this problem.
5. New orders of priests, called friars, were organised to instruct the people.
6. In 1209 St Francis founded the Friars Minor (little brothers) to work among the poor. In 1215 St Dominic founded the Order of Preachers to teach Church doctrine.
7. The friars owned nothing. They begged for their living. Their good example and their learning helped the Church to win back many who had fallen away.

F. Pilgrimages
1. Pilgrimages were very important during the Middle Ages and many people travelled across Europe visiting holy shrines, e.g. Rome, Santiago, Canterbury and Lough Derg.
2. (i) Pilgrims travelled along recognised routes and were able to stay at special pilgrim hostels. (ii) Where these were unavailable, guidebooks gave information on good and bad inns, local sites, etc.

Medieval Europe

3. Jerusalem was the most important pilgrim destination. Overland travel could take years and storms and pirates made travel by sea very dangerous. Muslims controlled Jerusalem and the Holy Land for most of the Middle Ages and from time to time they persecuted Christians.

4. The Church encouraged Europe's nobles to go on Crusade to win back the Holy Land from the Muslims. These wars were extremely vicious and ultimately failed.

MEDIEVAL SOCIETY: THOSE WHO LABOURED

A. *The Serfs*

1. During the Middle Ages most Europeans were serfs, i.e. they were unfree peasants 'tied to the land', with few rights.

2. (i) Serfs had to work whenever their lords demanded. (ii) They had to pay their lords many taxes and (iii) they had to have their approval whenever they married. (iv) Serfs had one important right: they could not be evicted from their land.

B. The Manor

1. Serfs lived on manors, i.e. self-contained farm-villages.
2. The arable land of each manor consisted of three great fields, each of which grew wheat, grew barley and then lay fallow according to a three-year rotation.

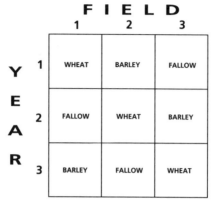

F I E L D

		1	2	3
Y	**1**	WHEAT	BARLEY	FALLOW
E A	**2**	FALLOW	WHEAT	BARLEY
R	**3**	BARLEY	FALLOW	WHEAT

THREE-FIELD ROTATION

3. Each serf cultivated strips of land in each field and thus shared in each crop.
4. Rough land on the edge of the village was used as common grazing. The surrounding forests provided fuel and game.
5. Serfs worked the fields cooperatively and each contributed a fixed amount of labour and equipment.
6. The reeve, who represented the serfs, and the bailiff, who represented the lord, decided on the details of the work.

An illumination from the Luttrell Psalter showing medieval peasants ploughing

C. How the People Lived

1. The serfs lived in timber-framed cottages with walls of wattle and daub, thatched roofs and mud floors.
2. A fire occupied the middle of the floor and there were a few crude stools and benches.

3. The people ate and drank from wooden bowls and cups.
4. Reeds and straw covered the floor and hid waste food, animal droppings, bones and vermin.

D. The End of Serfdom

1. The serfs often revolted against their living conditions.
2. They were frequently very inefficient workers.
3. From the fourteenth century onwards, therefore, many lords allowed their serfs to buy their freedom and replaced them with more efficient paid labourers.
4. Some serfs became free by escaping into the towns because the law decreed 'town air makes free'.

MEDIEVAL CITIES

A. Fall and Rise

1. Cities disappeared from many areas of Europe after the collapse of the Roman empire.
2. However, city life began to revive from c. 1000.
3. Some cities developed from earlier Roman ones – e.g. (i) Cologne where an archbishop ruled, (ii) Lyons at an important river crossing, (iii) Paris at an important trading centre, (iv) York on an easily defended site.
4. Others were built from scratch – (i) to encourage trade, e.g. Dublin, or (ii) to help with a military conquest, e.g. Caernarvon.

B. Appearance

1. Medieval cities were small and their growth was restricted because they were surrounded by defensive walls and moats.
2. Streets were narrow, twisting, unpaved and dirty.
3. Most buildings were multi-storey, timber-framed houses with wattle-and-daub walls. Roofs were thatched or tiled with wooden shingles.
4. To make the best use of space, upper storeys projected over the streets.
5. There was constant danger from fire and every night all citizens had to comply with a curfew, i.e. 'to cover the fire'.

C. The Guilds

1. Cities were important centres of trade and industry.
2. The craftsmen associated with each industry lived in the same district and their homes were their workshops.
3. The craftsmen were organised in guilds which regulated every aspect of their trade – training, prices, quality and working hours – so that nobody had an unfair advantage.

4. The guilds also looked after the social, economic and religious needs of their members, e.g. by helping members' widows and orphans, by setting up schools and hospitals and by taking part in religious festivals and miracle plays.

The Shambles, York. This is a typical narrow, twisting, medieval street.
Note the timber frames in the walls and the projecting upper storeys of the houses

D. Apprentice to Master

1. A craftsman began his training as an apprentice. As such, (i) he paid a fee to a master and (ii) lived in his house while (iii) he learned his trade.
2. After several years' training the guild examined the apprentice and if he reached a satisfactory standard, he became a journeyman, i.e. a qualified workman paid by the day.
3. A very skilled journeyman became a master-craftsman when he produced a masterpiece. Then, if he had enough money, he could open a workshop, take in apprentices and participate in running the guild.
4. In many cities, e.g. London, the trade guilds controlled the city council and elected the mayor.

E. Trade Fairs

1. Trade fairs took place in many cities as people from over a wide area gathered periodically to exchange goods.
2. These fairs had special pie-powder (dusty-feet) courts to prevent cheating and to punish thieves, vagabonds and forgers.

3. Sometimes groups of cities combined to form common markets, to trade among themselves and to exclude rivals – e.g. the Hanseatic League of north Germany and the Baltic.

F. Schools and Universities

1. During the Middle Ages most cathedrals had schools to educate those destined for important jobs in the Church.
2. Seven subjects, the seven liberal arts, were studied. These were grammar (Latin), rhetoric (public speaking), logic, arithmetic, geometry, astronomy and music.
3. Some schools developed into universities. Others were founded when students and teachers migrated to a city from another university. Migrants from Paris set up Oxford university c. 1249.
4. Few books were available during the Middle Ages and students had to try to memorise their lectures.
5. At the end of their course of studies, students took part in debates to test their knowledge and debating skills. Those reaching a sufficiently high standard received a degree.
6. Some students then studied for a doctorate.
7. Thus a student might study theology at Paris, law at Bologna or medicine at Salerno or Padua.
8. At first students lived in inns and lodging houses but because they were often rowdy, the university authorities forced them to live in special colleges. Sometimes wealthy patrons built these colleges, e.g. Robert Sorbonne, whose name became synonymous with the university of Paris.

G. The Black Death

1. Medieval cities were crowded and dirty. They had no sewers or waste-collection system. Rubbish piled up in the streets and became the home of rats and vermin.
2. As a result, there were many epidemics. The worst was the bubonic plague – the Black Death.
3. Fleas, carried on black rats, carried the plague virus. When a flea bit a human the virus entered the bloodstream.
4. Fever, swellings and death followed quickly.
5. In 1348 the Black Death killed 30 per cent of Europe's population. Some areas lost all their population. Others escaped entirely.
6. Few blamed the rats or the dirt. Instead, they blamed bad air, the Jews, their sins or God's anger.
7. Those who blamed the air tried to protect themselves with posies of flowers.
8. Those who blamed Jews killed them.
9. Those who blamed their own sins took part in religious processions, fasted and flogged themselves.

10. The plague troubled Europe for centuries but it was never again as severe. People had built up some immunity. The brown rat appeared in Europe and destroyed the black rat, the original carrier of the virus.

6 THE RENAISSANCE

THE BEGINNINGS OF THE RENAISSANCE

A. Definition
1. The word 'Renaissance' means 'rebirth'.
2. In history it refers to the period c. 1300–1650 when people (i) abandoned the art and culture of the Middle Ages and (ii) tried to create a new civilisation based on the art and culture of Greece and Rome.
3. There were also many important developments in science and vernacular literature.

B. Why the Renaissance began in Italy
1. The rulers of fourteenth-century Italy were too weak to re-create the political greatness of ancient Rome but they were rich enough to re-create some of its great culture.
2. The northern cities were centres of trade, industry and banking. Many of their wealthy rulers and merchants were interested in art for art's sake and they willingly patronised (sponsored) artists and writers.
3. Italy's libraries contained many Latin and Greek manuscripts, important sources of information on the ancient world.
4. The landscape was filled with ruins and statues which served as models for architects and artists.
5. Italy's universities were famous for the study of Roman law, which led students to become interested in Roman civilisation.

C. The Medici of Florence
1. Cosimo (1389–1464) and Lorenzo (1449–1492) de Medici were rich bankers and famous patrons.
2. They paid artists and scholars to settle and study in Florence and to decorate the city with great works of art.
3. They were so important in stimulating interest in literature, art and the classical world that many historians regard them as the originators of the Renaissance.

D. The Popes as Patrons

1. Rome had once been the magnificent capital of a great empire but by the 1300s much of the city was in ruins.
2. The popes wanted to rebuild the city in all its ancient magnificence to increase the prestige of the Church and to add to their personal glory.
3. Nicholas V was the first Renaissance pope. He (i) studied the classics, (ii) founded the Vatican Library and (iii) planned to rebuild Rome and St Peter's Basilica.
4. Sixtus IV built the Sistine Chapel and paid famous artists such as Botticelli to decorate it.
5. Julius II employed Bramante and Michelangelo to design St Peter's Basilica. Raphael decorated his private apartments while Michelangelo painted the ceiling of the Sistine Chapel and carved his magnificent tomb.

PRINTING

A. Manuscripts

During the Middle Ages, scribes wrote books by hand onto parchment or vellum. Books were therefore few and expensive.

B. Block Printing

1. Block printing was invented at the end of the Middle Ages.
2. Paper, made from rags, was also invented at this time.
3. Block printing involved: (i) carving an entire page of words onto a block of timber, (ii) inking it and (iii) pressing it onto the paper.
4. However, carving a page-block took a long time. The blocks wore out quickly and could be used for nothing else when a print run finished.

C. Johann Gutenberg (1400–1468)

1. Johann Gutenberg was born in Mainz.
2. He was a goldsmith and c. 1448 he invented movable metal type, i.e. he cast single letters in metal.
3. Words, sentences and pages could now be created by (i) assembling the individual letters, (ii) locking them in a frame, (iii) inking them and (iv) pressing paper onto the metal type.
4. When they finished a piece of work, the printers unlocked the frame and used the letters to compose new pages.
5. Gutenberg's greatest achievement was the forty-two-line Bible, still considered to be the most beautiful book ever printed.

D. The Spread of Printing
1. Printing spread quickly.
2. William Caxton set up England's first press in 1476.
3. In Venice Aldus Manutius produced many cheap but beautiful editions of the Latin and Greek classics. They were the first books printed for a large market and are the forerunners of the modern paperback.

E. The Importance of Printing
1. When books had to be handwritten, a fire, a flood or a mouse could destroy months of writing and years of research in a few minutes. Those days were now gone and printing allowed books to be produced quickly and cheaply.
2. It was now much easier to become literate.
3. Religious and political ideas and geographical, scientific and medical knowledge could now spread quickly and widely.
4. Books helped to create the standard versions of most European languages.

HUMANISM

A. The Humanists
1. Scholars interested in the ancient civilisations of Greece and Rome were called humanists because they believed that their knowledge would make them better people, i.e. more humane.
2. Important humanists included Petrarch, Boccaccio, Machiavelli and More.

B. Francesco Petrarch (1304–1374)
1. Petrarch collected many ancient manuscripts and became famous for his great learning.
2. He composed many works in Latin but he is best remembered for his *Canzoniere*, a collection of love poems in Italian dedicated to Laura, a girl he had once seen but never met.
3. Petrarch also invented the sonnet.

C. Giovanni Boccaccio (1313–1375)
1. Boccaccio was also a famous collector of manuscripts and a Latin scholar.
2. The *Decameron* is his best-known book.
3. Written in Italian, the *Decameron* contains 100 stories told by a group of Florentines seeking refuge from the Black Death in a country villa.
4. These stories are considered to be the earliest examples of the modern short story.

D. Niccolò Machiavelli (1469–1527)

1. Niccolò Machiavelli was a Florentine diplomat and he wrote one of the most famous political books of all time, *The Prince*.
2. According to Machiavelli, a successful ruler should be unscrupulous and should act brutally or kindly, honestly or dishonestly, as the situation demanded.
3. *The Prince* earned Machiavelli a reputation for evil and his nickname 'Old Nick' became associated with the devil.

E. Thomas More (1478–1535)

1. More was a lawyer and became Henry VIII's lord chancellor.
2. More was famous for his scholarship, wit, kindness and holiness.
3. His friends included the great scholar Erasmus and the great artist Holbein.
4. He was very interested in education and his daughter, Margaret Roper, was one of the most learned women of the age.
5. (i) His *History of King Richard III* is the first modern history book in English. (ii) His book *Utopia* is a satire on the politics of his time and it describes what a country should be – peaceful, prosperous, hard-working and tolerant.
6. More refused to accept Henry VIII as head of the Church.
7. He was imprisoned in the Tower of London where he wrote A *Dialogue of Comfort Against Tribulations*.
8. He was beheaded in 1535 declaring, 'I die the king's good servant, but God's first.'

F. Vernacular Writing

Humanists encouraged scholars to use Greek and Latin but ordinary people continued to use their vernacular (everyday) languages and many writers used them to produce great works of literature. Miguel Cervantes was such a writer.

G. Miguel de Cervantes Saavedra (1547–1616)

1. Cervantes was born at Alcala in Spain. He was seriously wounded in the battle of Lepanto (1570).
2. Later he was enslaved by pirates and had to be ransomed.
3. He became a tax-collector, but was imprisoned because he did not collect enough money.
4. According to tradition, he began his famous novel *Don Quixote* while he was in prison.
5. Don Quixote is a mad, idealistic old knight who travels through Spain righting wrongs and helping the poor and weak.
6. He and his worldly-wise, cynical servant Sancho Panza become embroiled in many adventures.
7. The most famous is probably the one in which he mistakes windmills for giants.

8. Cervantes used the novel to comment on life and his book presents a marvellous portrait of sixteenth-century Spain.

9. Cervantes also wrote many plays and poems but Don Quixote remains his most memorable creation. Indeed the Don has entered the English language: a good, eccentric person who attempts the impossible is often described as 'quixotic'.

ART AND ARTISTS OF THE RENAISSANCE

A. Medieval Painting

Medieval paintings were very different from those of the Renaissance.

1. They were usually flat and lifeless.
2. They did not show proportion correctly.
3. They were chiefly concerned with religious ideas.

B. Renaissance Painting

Renaissance artists used various techniques to make their pictures as lifelike as possible.

1. They used perspective to give their paintings depth.
2. Many studied anatomy to make their paintings more lifelike.
3. Most used oil-based paints to give their colours solidity and depth.
4. Some created frescoes, i.e. paintings done on wet plaster.
5. Many artists were portrait-painters.
6. Artists painted nude figures, especially in pictures illustrating Greek and Roman myths.

C. Sculpture

1. Medieval sculptors did not show the human form accurately. Their statues were usually decorations carved on walls.
2. Renaissance sculptors produced free-standing statues and studied anatomy to make them anatomically correct.

D. Medieval Architecture

1. Medieval cathedrals were designed on a huge scale to show the greatness of God and the unimportance of mankind. They were noted for their pointed Gothic arches and their lavish decoration.
2. The castles of the great lords were large, uncomfortable and mostly ugly.
3. The houses of the people were generally small, uncomfortable and mostly ugly.

E. Renaissance Architects

1. Renaissance architects such as Brunelleschi and Palladio designed buildings on a more human scale.

'The Marriage of the Virgin' by Raphael. This is a typical Renaissance painting. Note the balance in the picture with the group of people in the foreground and the building in the background; the two groups of people balance at each side of the painting; the use of perspective and the symmetrically structured building with its round Romanesque arches

2. They based their work on the writings of the Roman Vetruvius Pollio and on the ruins of Roman buildings.
    3. Palladio designed villas which were much more comfortable than the rough feudal castles they replaced.
    4. Renaissance architects also designed churches and palaces based on Roman buildings.
    5. Brunelleschi designed Florence Cathedral, giving it the largest dome since the Romans built the Pantheon in AD 118.

F. Leonardo da Vinci (1452–1519)

1. Leonardo da Vinci was born near Florence in 1452.
2. Very early in his life Leonardo showed a great talent for art and in 1470 his father sent him to study with Andrea Verrocchio, one of Florence's finest artists.
3. Leonardo left Florence in 1482 and later worked in Milan, Rome, Venice, Mantua and France, where he died.
4. Few paintings survive which are undoubtedly his. These include 'The Virgin of the Rocks', 'The Last Supper' and the 'Mona Lisa'.
5. Leonardo used a painting technique called 'sfumato' in which figures and backgrounds blend into one another.
6. Leonardo rarely finished any of his paintings – he was always anxious to get on with some new project.
7. Many of his pictures deteriorated very quickly. He often experimented with new paints, varnishes or plasters and they didn't always work very well.
8. Leonardo always carried a notebook. Some five thousand pages survive, filled with drawings of plants, animals, dissections, and inventions including a hang-glider, a submarine, a parachute, a tank and a multiple cannon. His notes were often written in 'mirror writing'.

Caricature drawings by Leonardo da Vinci

G. Michelangelo Buonarroti (1475–1564)

1. Michelangelo was born near Florence in 1475.
2. His talent as a sculptor brought him to the notice of Lorenzo de Medici, who had him educated in his own household.

Self-portrait by Michelangelo

3. Michelangelo left Florence when Lorenzo died but often returned, though he spent most of his life in Rome.
4. Michelangelo loved sculpture more than any other art-form. His most famous works include the 'Pietà' (1479) and 'David' (1505). The 'Pietà' is probably the finest representation of the crucified Christ ever made, and 'David' (five metres high) represents at once the smallness and greatness of Florence.
5. Pope Julius II called Michelangelo to Rome in 1503 to design his tomb. Michelangelo and the pope often quarrelled. Artists and cardinals plotted against him. Money was withheld and Michelangelo was diverted to other projects. He spent many years working on the tomb but never finished it.
6. From 1508 to 1512 Michelangelo painted the ceiling of the Sistine Chapel. He had to carry out most of the work lying on his back within inches of the ceiling. When it was finished, it told the story of the Old Testament from the Creation to Noah. The ceiling is currently being cleaned and once more we can see the great fresco in all its glory.
7. In 1538 Michelangelo began designing the dome for the new St Peter's Basilica. He devoted himself to this work until his death in 1564.
8. Michelangelo was a fine poet as well as a painter, a sculptor and an architect. He was, in other words, a true Renaissance man – an all-round genius.

H. Albrecht Dürer (1471–1528)

1. Albrecht Dürer was born in Nuremberg.
2. He was a goldsmith, an engraver and an artist.
3. He visited Italy and studied the work of all the great artists. Their influence is shown in his self-portraits and in 'The Madonna of the Rose Garlands' and 'Four Apostles'.
4. Dürer is best remembered for his woodcuts and engravings, many on religious themes.
5. Dürer was a great traveller and he made many drawings and water-colours on his journeys. They show animals, plants, landscapes and people, all depicted with great precision.

Self-portrait by Albrecht Dürer. Note the use of the window and landscape to suggest depth and the artist's initials, A.D.

THE SCIENTIFIC REVOLUTION

A. Medieval and Renaissance Science

1. During the Middle Ages, people took most of their scientific ideas from the Bible or from the writings of Aristotle.
2. However, Renaissance people refused to accept ideas simply because others had believed them for a long time.
3. Instead, they investigated ideas to discover whether they were true or false, and carried out experiments and made careful observations to find out about the world and nature.

B. Astronomy

1. During the Middle Ages most people believed that the earth was the centre of the universe and that the sun and all the planets revolved around it.
2. A Polish astronomer, Nicholas Copernicus, concluded that the earth and the planets revolved around the sun.
3. Many people, Catholics and Protestants alike, objected to this theory as it seemed to contradict the Bible.

C. Galileo Galilei (1564–1642)

1. Galileo was born in Pisa, where he became professor of mathematics in 1589.
2. By then he had discovered that the pendulum could be used to measure time exactly, and that objects fall at the same speed irrespective of their weight.
3. He invented a thermometer and he perfected the refracting telescope.
4. His work with this instrument convinced him that the moon's surface consisted of hills, valleys and craters and that it reflected the light of the sun.
5. He declared that the Milky Way contained innumerable stars.
6. He discovered four of Jupiter's moons and also sunspots.
7. He supported Copernicus's theories but in 1633 the Inquisition (a Church court) forced him to retract his views as they seemed to contradict the Bible. He was kept under house arrest for the remainder of his life.
8. However, he continued his scientific research although he was now old and blind. Because of his many discoveries, Galileo has been called 'The Father of Modern Science'.
9. In 1992 the Church admitted that the verdict at Galileo's trial had been incorrect.

D. Galen (130–201) and Andreas Vesalius (1514–1564)

1. Galen was the most important medical writer of the ancient world and his book on anatomy was used in medical schools for many centuries.
2. However, Galen based his ideas on animal dissections because the Romans (and later the Christian Church) forbade the dissection of humans. Many of his ideas were incorrect and no proper breakthrough in medicine could take place until these wrong ideas were put right.
3. Andreas Vesalius was born in Brussels in 1514 and became a professor of medicine in Padua, then the centre of medical education in Europe.
4. In 1543 he published his book *On the Fabric of the Human Body*, which he based on the careful dissection of human bodies.
5. This book greatly advanced the science of anatomy because of its excellent descriptions and detailed drawings.
6. The Inquisition sentenced Vesalius to death for 'body-snatching' and for dissecting human remains. However, the sentence was commuted to a pilgrimage to Jerusalem. Vesalius died on the journey home.

BACKGROUND

A. The World Picture c. 1400
1.   In 1400 few people knew much about the world outside their own immediate area.
2.   However, many sailors had a good knowledge of the Atlantic and Mediterranean coasts of Europe.
3.   Some scholars knew about China from the writings of Marco Polo, who had visited that country in the 1300s.
4.   A few people believed that there were lands across the Atlantic.
5.   Many scholars and sailors knew that the world was a sphere.
6.   Most people thought that the world was flat. This idea was reflected in the 'mappae mundi', i.e. maps of the world drawn at the time.

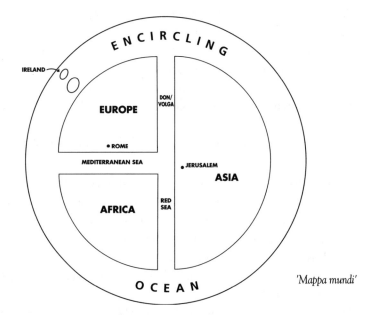

'Mappa mundi'

B. Difficulties
Long-distance travel was very difficult at this time.
1.   Roads were bad which made travel very slow.
2.   Bandits, outlaws, pirates and wars made travel unsafe.
3.   Few ships were strong enough to sail in very stormy waters.
4.   Sailing ships depended on winds, which were often unreliable.
5.   There were no accurate navigational instruments to guide sailors.

C. Means

This situation changed in the 1400s.

1. New types of ships, e.g. caravels, carracks and naos, were built with clinker planking to stand up to the storms of the Atlantic. They also had lateen (triangular) sails to sail close to, i.e. against, the wind.

Model of the Santa Maria. *Note the square sails on the fore and main masts and the lateen sail on the mizzen mast*

2. New navigational instruments, e.g. the astrolabe and the quadrant, became available to help sailors establish their latitude. Compasses helped them to find their direction and logs were used to calculate speed.

An astrolabe. Note the degrees marked along its edge

D. Motives

Many factors encouraged the explorers to sail.

1. They wished to spread Christianity among non-believers.
2. Some wanted to become rich by finding trade routes that would lead them to the 'Spice Islands' (Moluccas).
3. Others wanted to conquer new lands.
4. More wanted to become wealthy through capturing slaves or discovering gold.
5. Others wished to become famous for remarkable deeds.
6. A few were interested in gaining knowledge for its own sake.

THE EXPLORERS

A. The Portuguese Explorers

1. Prince Henry the Navigator set up a school and library for navigators at Cape Sagres (c. 1415) and sponsored voyages along the African coast. He hoped to find a routeway to India to give him control of the spice trade. He also wished to contact Prester John, a legendary Christian king in Africa, with whom he hoped to fight against the Muslims. By 1460, when Henry died, his ships had reached Sierra Leone.
2. Bartolomeo Dias rounded the Cape of Good Hope and entered the Indian Ocean in 1487.
3. Disguised as an Arab, Pedro de Covilhao explored the northern shores of the Indian Ocean and sent reports of his discoveries back to Portugal (1487–90).
4. At the same time, Portuguese sailors discovered the pattern of winds and currents in the Atlantic.
5. Using this information, Vasco da Gama sailed from Portugal to the Cape in record time. He sailed to Malindi in east Africa and on to Calicut in India, a centre of the spice trade. He fought with the local ruler, lost most of his ships and most of his crews on the voyage but the spices he brought home earned enormous profits for the Portuguese government (1497–9).

B. The Spanish Explorers

1. Spaniards were too involved in wars at home to take part in the explorations until their victory over the Muslims in 1492.
2. In the same year the Spanish government gave Christopher Columbus three ships to travel to Asia by sailing westwards across the Atlantic.
3. He based his voyage on calculations which made the world smaller and Asia bigger than they are and which put Cypangu (Japan) a thirty-day voyage westwards from Europe.
4. Columbus discovered numerous islands on this voyage, and on his three later voyages he discovered many more, together with part of the mainland of South America.

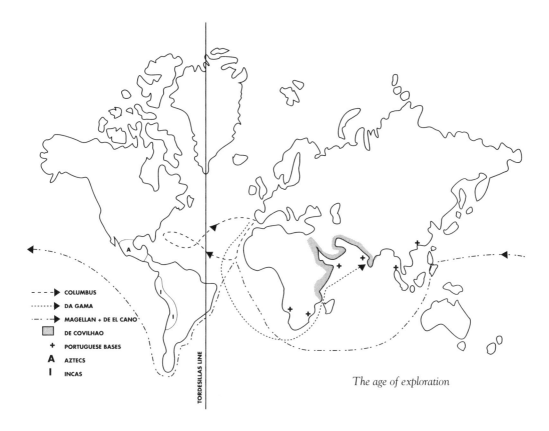

COLUMBUS
DA GAMA
MAGELLAN + DE EL CANO
DE COVILHAO
+ PORTUGUESE BASES
A AZTECS
I INCAS

TORDESILLAS LINE

The age of exploration

5.   He died in 1506 still believing that he had reached Asia, but puzzled and disappointed because he had not encountered the rich civilisations of India, China and Japan.

C. A New World

1.   An Italian sailor, Amerigo Vespucci, realised that Columbus had discovered a 'new world'.
2.   He wrote a pamphlet on the subject and was recognised as 'the intellectual discoverer of the New World'.
3.   Vasco Nunez de Balboa crossed the Isthmus of Panama in 1513 and discovered the Pacific Ocean, thus proving Vespucci's theories correct.

D. The Treaty of Tordesillas (1494)

To avoid conflict between their sailors, the Spanish and Portuguese governments agreed in the Treaty of Tordesillas to divide the world between them. Spain received most of the Americas. Portugal received Brazil, Africa and most of Asia.

E. Ferdinand Magellan (1480–1521)

1. Ferdinand Magellan, a Portuguese officer, believed that the Moluccas lay in Spain's half of the world.
2. In 1519 Charles V gave him five ships and 287 men to sail to the Moluccas by travelling around America in order to avoid seas that were controlled by the Portuguese.
3. Major incidents on the voyage included: (i) the winter of 1520–1 spent at Port St Julian when a ship was wrecked and sailors mutinied; (ii) the thirty-eight-day passage through the Magellan Strait when a ship deserted; (iii) the three-month crossing of the Pacific when seventeen men died of scurvy; (iv) the killing of Magellan in the Philippines.
4. Sebastian de el Cano now became fleet commander and he finally reached the Moluccas.
5. De el Cano took a cargo of spice on board the *Victoria*. The *Trinidad* tried to sail to Panama but had to return to the Moluccas, where the Portuguese captured it.
6. De el Cano sailed the *Victoria* across the Indian Ocean and around the Cape to Spain.
7. Only one ship and seventeen men survived of the fleet that set sail with Magellan. However, the spices more than paid the expenses of the voyage.
8. Historically and geographically the voyage is important as the first circumnavigation (sailing around) of the world.

THE CONQUISTADORES

A. Conquistadores

Spanish soldiers called conquistadores occupied and colonised America. The most famous were Hernando Cortés in Mexico and Francisco Pizarro in Peru.

B. Hernando Cortés (1485–1547)

1. Cortés and a tiny army landed in Mexico in 1519 and marched on Tenochtitlan, the capital of the Aztec empire.
2. At first the Aztecs were frightened by his steel weapons, guns and horses and Cortés captured their emperor, Montezuma.
3. However, the Aztecs rose against the Spaniards when Cortés tried to stop their human sacrifices. Montezuma was killed and the Spaniards had to flee Tenochtitlan.
4. Cortés collected more soldiers and Indian allies. He besieged Tenochtitlan and captured it (1521) thus gaining a huge empire for Spain.

C. Francisco Pizarro (1475–1541)

1. Pizarro landed in Peru in 1530.
2. He kidnapped Atahualpa, ruler of the Inca empire, and had him strangled.

3. His action so horrified the Indians that they offered little resistance to the Spaniards.

D. The Portuguese Conquistadores

1. Unlike the Spaniards, the Portuguese were opposed by numerous, highly developed peoples and they were therefore unable to establish a great land empire.
2. Instead, commanders like Affonso de Albuquerque captured important ports on the coasts of Africa and Asia. They used these ports as bases and used the superior strength of their warships to control the trade of the Indian Ocean.

E. The Spanish Empire

1. The Spanish conquistadores owned huge estates.
2. They kept cattle, grew cotton and sugar cane and dug for gold and silver.
3. At first they enslaved the Indians, many of whom died. Then the Spanish government passed many laws to protect them, though these were often ignored by the conquistadores.
4. The Spaniards imported African slaves to take the place of the Indians they could no longer use.
5. Missionaries worked hard to spread the Catholic religion among the Indians and were very successful.
6. They also protected the Indians from ruthless settlers and traders. In Paraguay the Jesuits set up Reductions – huge, self-contained estates where no Europeans were allowed. However, the Jesuits failed to make the Indians self-reliant and when the Jesuits were suppressed (1773), the Reductions disintegrated.

F. The Impact on Europe

1. Many Europeans emigrated to America and established colonies there, thus increasing the power and influence of their homelands.
2. Huge amounts of gold and silver flowed into Europe.
3. Prices rose causing great hardship to the poor.
4. New kinds of food, drink and drugs, e.g. potatoes, tea and tobacco, were imported into Europe and became part of the people's way of life.

G. The Impact on the Colonies

1. Great numbers of American Indians were killed or died from European diseases.
2. Their civilisations were almost totally destroyed.
3. The Indians became Christian and adopted European customs and languages.
4. Their standards of living fell dramatically and they came under the control of European masters.

BACKGROUND

A. Introduction

The word 'Reformation' refers to the break-up of the Catholic Church in the sixteenth century and to the growth of Protestant Christianity.

B. The State of the Church

There were numerous defects in the Catholic Church at the beginning of the sixteenth century.

1. Many people were very superstitious.
2. Many priests were badly trained or illiterate and few knew enough about religion to preach.
3. Many bishops were absentees, i.e. they did not live or work in their dioceses. Others were pluralists, i.e. they were in charge of several dioceses and did not take proper care of any of them.
4. Some men became popes by simony, i.e. by bribing the cardinals to elect them. Such popes were often more interested in politics, pleasure or art than in religion and they frequently neglected their duties.
5. Others got important jobs in the Church through nepotism, i.e. because they were related to an influential noble or clergyman.
6. Some monasteries and convents were very rich and many monks and nuns were more interested in wealth and comfort than in religion.

C. Improvements

There were also individuals and groups who worked to improve the Church.

1. Cardinal Ximenes of Spain founded the university of Alcala (1508) to train priests and he sponsored a modern translation of the Bible.
2. New orders such as the Capuchins and the Brethren of the Common Life worked to educate the poor.

D. The Renaissance

The Renaissance greatly influenced the Reformation.

1. Reformers used printed books to spread their ideas quickly throughout Europe. Thus, while heretics (those who rejected Church doctrine) could be executed, their ideas, once in print, could not be destroyed.
2. Their studies of the ancient world showed many scholars how badly the Church had declined since the time of the apostles. This led them to demand improvements.

3. People like Thomas More and Erasmus wanted changes to come from within the Church. Others, such as Luther and Calvin, believed that the Church was too corrupt to improve itself. They therefore set up their own reformed Churches.

MARTIN LUTHER

A. Martin Luther (1483–1546)

Martin Luther was born in the German state of Saxony. He became an Augustinian friar and was appointed professor of Bible at Wittenberg university (1509).

Martin Luther

B. The Ninety-Five Theses

1. In October 1517 friar John Tetzel was selling indulgences near Wittenberg. Tetzel declared that souls in purgatory went to heaven as soon as he received money on their behalf.
2. Luther was furious at the idea that people could buy a place in heaven. He condemned Tetzel and abuses in the Church in ninety-five theses (ideas for debate) which he nailed to the door of the local church.
3. The theses were printed and passed around Germany. Luther became a hero almost overnight for he had complained about abuses that others had feared to discuss.
4. Later Luther denied that the pope had any special authority in the Church.

C. Condemnation

1. Pope Leo X condemned Luther's ideas and excommunicated him.
2. The German Diet (parliament) meeting at Worms outlawed Luther when he refused to give up his beliefs (1521).
3. However, Luther's overlord, the elector of Saxony, protected him and he spent the rest of his life in Wittenberg translating the Bible into German, writing, teaching and organising his Church.

D. Ideas

The following are some of Luther's main ideas.

1. The Bible is the only means by which God reveals himself.
2. Salvation comes by faith alone in Jesus Christ.
3. There are only two sacraments, Baptism and the Eucharist.
4. The mass is not a sacrifice but only commemorates the Last Supper.
5. Christ is present *with* the bread and wine in the Eucharist.
6. Everyone should receive bread and wine at holy communion.
7. Religious services should be in the vernacular.
8. Priests should be allowed to marry. (Luther married an ex-nun, Katharina von Bora.)
9. Each ruler should be head of the Church in their own state.

E. The Spread of Lutheranism

1. Many north German princes became Lutherans and forced their people to follow them. They now had more control over their people and enriched themselves with confiscated Church lands.
2. However, most of those who became Lutherans did so because they found Luther's ideas satisfying and convincing.

F. The Peasants' Revolt

Germany's downtrodden peasants thought that they could successfully defy their masters as Luther had successfully defied the pope. They rebelled (1525) and Luther encouraged the princes to slaughter them, which they did by the thousand.

G. War and a Peace

1. Emperor Charles V and southern German rulers formed the Holy League to stop Luther's ideas spreading into their lands.
2. Lutheran princes formed the Schmalkaldic League to resist a Catholic attack.
3. War broke out in 1546. It dragged on until 1555 by which time it was clear that neither side could win.
4. According to the Peace of Augsburg which ended the war each ruler could decide the religion of their people (*cuius regio eius religio*).
5. However, as the Peace applied to Catholics and Lutherans only, trouble was bound to arise with Calvinists and other religious groups that had developed in the meantime.

JOHN CALVIN

A. John Calvin (1509–1564)

John Calvin was a French Protestant who settled in Geneva, where he became leader of the local Protestant Church (1541).

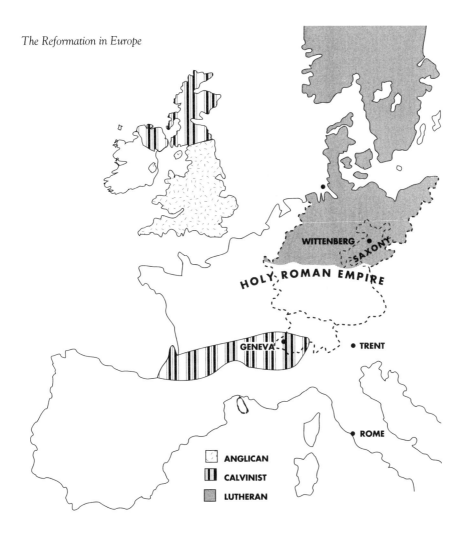

The Reformation in Europe

ANGLICAN
CALVINIST
LUTHERAN

B. Calvin's Ideas

Most of Calvin's ideas are contained in his book *The Institutes of the Christian Religion*. The following are among them.

1. The Bible is the final authority in religious matters.
2. Baptism and the Eucharist are the only sacraments.
3. The bread and wine do *not* change at the consecration and Christ is *not* present in the Eucharist.
4. From the beginning of time, God has predestined (chosen) some people for heaven and others for hell. The elect (saved) would be recognised by their good behaviour. Those destined for hell would be obvious by their bad behaviour.
5. Members of Calvin's Church would know for certain that they had been saved.

John Calvin

C. The Church in Geneva

1. The Consistory, a group of ministers and elders, controlled the Church in Geneva.
2. The ministers taught religion and led church services.
3. The elders supervised the people and informed the city government about wrongdoers who should be punished.
4. The citizens of Geneva elected the elders and the city government and, though Calvin had a lot of personal influence, final control over the Church lay with the citizens.
5. Geneva had excellent health, education and welfare services and a strong police force kept law and order. Geneva was so well run that many believed it to be 'the city of God on Earth' in contrast to Rome, the devil's city.

D. The Spread of Calvinism

1. Calvinism became very popular because it gave people the certainty of salvation and control over their local Church.
2. Highly trained missionaries, e.g. John Knox, educated at Calvin's university of Geneva, travelled throughout Europe preaching Calvin's ideas.
3. Calvin's printing press produced numerous books and pamphlets in many languages explaining his ideas and attacking his enemies.

THE ANGLICAN REFORMATION

A. Henry VIII (1491–1547)

1. At first Henry VIII opposed Protestantism, and Pope Leo X gave him the title 'Defender of the Faith' when he wrote a pamphlet attacking Luther.
2. Henry married Catherine of Aragon in 1509 but only one of their children lived, Princess Mary. Henry feared that a woman would never be able to control England's nobles and by 1533 it was clear that Catherine could have no more children.
3. Henry therefore asked Pope Clement VII to annul his marriage so that he could marry Anne Boleyn. The pope was then virtually a prisoner of Emperor Charles V, Catherine's nephew, and he ignored Henry's requests.
4. However, Thomas Cranmer, the archbishop of Canterbury, annulled the marriage and Henry married Anne Boleyn (1533).
5. In 1534 parliament passed the Act of Supremacy, which made Henry head of the Church of England (the Anglican Church).

Henry VIII

B. The Suppression of the Monasteries

1. Henry was always very short of money. He therefore used his powers as head of the Church to suppress (shut down) the monasteries and convents and to confiscate their wealth.
2. He sold their lands cheaply to the nobility and gentry, who became strong supporters of Henry's Anglican Church.
3. Very few monks or nuns objected to the suppression. All received pensions and many continued to work as parish clergy.

C. The Anglican Church Finally Established

1. Henry made few obvious changes in the Church.
2. The mass was still celebrated in Latin and Lutherans were executed, as were those few, e.g. Thomas More and John Fisher, who remained loyal to the pope.
3. However, a Bible in English was placed in every church.

4. Henry's successor, Edward VI (his son by Jane Seymour), was a convinced Protestant. He (i) replaced the Latin missal with the English Book of Common Prayer, (ii) replaced the mass with a Protestant service in English and (iii) allowed priests to marry.

5. Edward died in 1553 and his Catholic half-sister, Mary, became queen. Mary tried to restore Catholicism but her savage persecution of ordinary folk who were Protestants turned most English people against her and the Catholic Church.

D. Elizabeth I (1533–1603)

1. Mary's half-sister, Elizabeth (the daughter of Anne Boleyn), now became queen (1558).

2. Elizabeth did not want religious conflict in England. She set up a compromise Church which had many Protestant doctrines mixed in with Catholic ceremonies.

3. Everyone had to attend Sunday service or else pay a heavy fine. However, Elizabeth did not begin to persecute Catholics until 1570, when Pope Pius V excommunicated her and encouraged English Catholics to rebel.

4. This action by the pope led many English Catholics to join the Anglican Church to show their loyalty to their queen.

THE CATHOLIC (COUNTER-) REFORMATION

A. The Catholic Reformation

The Catholic or Counter-Reformation was an attempt by the Catholic Church (i) to end these abuses which had caused the Protestant Reformation, (ii) to overthrow Protestantism and (iii) to spread the Catholic religion world-wide.

B. Reforming Popes

1. Popes such as Alexander VI and Julius II had given great scandal. However, beginning with Paul III a new line of good-living popes made many improvements in the Church.

2. Pius V (1504–72) was the most famous. (i) He ended corruption in Rome and imprisoned all who failed to live up to his standards. (ii) He encouraged Catholic rulers to persecute Protestants. (iii) He ordered England's Catholics to rebel against Elizabeth I. (iv) He enforced the decrees of the Council of Trent. (v) He helped to organise new religious orders to fight Protestantism.

C. The Council of Trent

1. The Council of Trent (1545–63) was a meeting of Catholic bishops held to solve the problems created by the Reformation.

2. The Council restated the traditional doctrines of the Church. (i) Faith and good

works are needed for salvation. (ii) The Bible *and* tradition contain Christ's teachings. (iii) The bread and wine *become* the body and blood of Christ at the consecration of the mass. (iv) The mass is a sacrifice. (v) There are seven sacraments.

3. The Council also issued orders to improve discipline within the Church. (i) Clergymen must live among their people. (ii) Priests were to be educated in seminaries. (iii) There was to be a catechism to instruct the clergy. (iv) An Index of Forbidden Books was to be compiled. (v) Simony, nepotism, pluralism and the marriage of clergy were outlawed.

4. Protestants rejected the religious ideas of the Council and so the Christian Churches became more divided.

5. However, standards improved within the Catholic Church as members accepted the Council's decrees on discipline.

D. The Society of Jesus

Many religious orders were founded to deal with the Reformation. The Society of Jesus (Jesuits) was the most important.

1. Ignatius of Loyola (1491–1556), a Spanish soldier, experienced a conversion to Christ while recovering from war wounds.

2. In 1534 he founded the Society of Jesus. Organised like an army, its members were highly trained as teachers and preachers and they took a special vow of obedience to the pope.

3. Jesuits worked as missionaries in Asia and America.

4. They set up (the best) schools in Europe.

5. They won back central Europe to the Catholic Church.

6. Jesuits became advisers to princes and kings.

7. They were regarded as the spearhead of the Counter-Reformation.

E. The Spanish Inquisition

1. The Spanish Inquisition was a court set up to keep the Catholic religion dominant in Spain.

2. The Inquisition questioned anyone denounced as a heretic.

3. It released those it believed innocent but tortured those it suspected to be Protestants until they admitted their 'guilt'.

4. Such people were released if they recanted (gave up their beliefs).

5. They were burned to death at a public auto-da-fé (act of faith) if they did not.

6. We would consider the Inquisition's methods barbaric but it is important to remember that it operated more fairly than most other court systems functioning at the time.

7. The Inquisition destroyed Protestantism in Spain but its secrecy and informers created an atmosphere of fear and suspicion that lasted until it was finally abolished in 1820.

8. The power of the Inquisition was absolute and it imprisoned important churchmen as well as writers, government officials and poor peasants.

Auto-da-fé. Note the penitential dress worn by the victims

IRELAND AND THE REFORMATION

A. The State of the Church

The Church in Ireland was very corrupt at the beginning of the sixteenth century.

1. Irish chiefs or English kings appointed bishops, almost always for political or family reasons.
2. Few priests were educated.
3. The ordinary people were either superstitious or did not care about religion.
4. However, Franciscan friars were very popular and influential in some parts of the country.
5. Priests with a Gaelic background frequently quarrelled with priests from an English background. These quarrels often led to fighting.

B. The Anglican Reformation

The Tudors brought the Reformation to Ireland but the Anglican Church had little success.

1. There were very few Protestant missionaries and very few of these could preach to the people in Irish.
2. Later, Protestantism became associated with the English conquest and people were unwilling to accept Protestantism because by doing so they were accepting English control.
3. From the 1550s onwards, Irish Catholic priests, trained in the ideals of the Counter-Reformation, began to work in the country and convinced the people to remain in the Catholic Church.

C. Calvinism

Scottish Presbyterians brought Calvinism to northern Ireland during the Ulster plantation and later French Huguenot refugees brought Calvinism to the south and east of the country.

THE FIRST PLANTATIONS

A. An Incomplete Conquest

1. The Normans who first invaded Ireland in 1169 were never strong enough to conquer the country completely.
2. The Gaelic Irish, on the other hand, were never strong enough or united enough to expel them.
3. Cut off from England, the descendants of the Norman invaders adopted many Irish customs and intermarried with Irish families.
4. By 1485, when Henry VII became the first Tudor king, only the Pale, a small area around Dublin, was inhabited by 'the king's loyal English subjects'.
5. Garret Mór Fitzgerald, the earl of Kildare, disliked Henry and tried (unsuccessfully) to overthrow him. Self-preservation now forced the Tudors to become involved in Ireland.

B. The Tudors

1. Henry VII brought the Kildare Fitzgeralds under control. Henry VIII (1537) wiped them out but he also tried to establish friendly relations with the Gaelic chiefs.
2. His daughter Mary introduced a new policy, the policy of plantation. This involved taking land from the Irish and giving it to English settlers.

C. Aims

All the plantations aimed: (i) to punish Irish rebels; (ii) to make future rebellion impossible; (iii) to enrich the king's servants and friends; and (iv) to Anglicise Ireland, i.e. to make it like England.

D. The Laois/Offaly Plantation (1556)

1. The O'Moores and O'Connors of Laois/Offaly often raided the Pale.
2. Queen Mary's army drove them into the west of the region.
3. The government gave the rest to English settlers.
4. The settlers farmed the land in the English manner.
5. They built garrison towns at Maryborough (Portlaoise) and Phillipstown (Daingean).
6. Sheriffs were appointed to administer English law.
7. The settlers brought in some tenants from England but they also employed Irish labourers.

8. At first the plantation seemed successful. However, there were never enough English settlers and the native Irish overwhelmed the plantation during the Nine Years' War (1594–1603).

E. The Desmond Rebellion

1. The Fitzgeralds of Desmond survived much longer than their cousins in Kildare.
2. However, they rebelled (1579) when Elizabeth's officials tried to make them submit to English authority.
3. Munster was devastated in the war that followed and all the Fitzgerald lands were confiscated.

F. The Munster Plantation (1586)

1. Elizabeth divided this land into seigniories (large estates).
2. She then gave them to undertakers at very low rents. (Undertakers were so called because they undertook certain responsibilities.)
3. They promised: (i) to bring in English tenants; (ii) to build defences; (iii) to cultivate the land in the English manner and (iv) to provide soldiers to defend the plantation.
4. Important planters included the explorer Walter Raleigh and the poet Edmund Spenser.
5. The venture prospered but the planters neglected their defences and the plantation was nearly wiped out during the Nine Years' War.
6. However, it restarted in the 1600s and adventurers like Richard Boyle grew immensely rich by exploiting the resources of the region.
7. Thus, the first attempt to plant Munster failed. The second succeeded.

THE ULSTER PLANTATION

A. Background

1. In 1594 Hugh O'Neill, earl of Tyrone, began the Nine Years' War in order to preserve his independence from English control.
2. He was defeated at Kinsale in 1601 and in 1603 he surrendered to the English at Mellifont. O'Neill was allowed to keep his great estates in Tyrone but in 1607 he and many of the Gaelic nobility of Ulster fled to Europe.
3. The government declared them traitors and confiscated their lands in six Ulster counties (Donegal, Coleraine, Tyrone, Fermanagh, Armagh, Cavan).

B. The Scheme of Plantation

The Ulster plantation was much better organised than previous ones. The land was divided between undertakers, servitors and deserving Irish as follows.

	Undertakers	Servitors	Deserving Irish
Estates	2,000 acres	1,500 acres	1,000 acres
Rent	£10.65	£12.00	£10.65
Tenants	English & Scottish	English, Scottish & Irish	Irish
Buildings	Castle	Enclosure (bawn)	Stone house

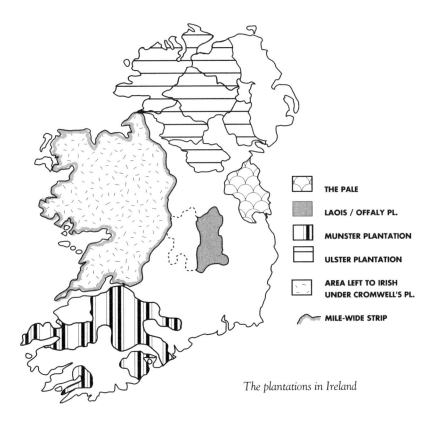

Legend:
- THE PALE
- LAOIS / OFFALY PL.
- MUNSTER PLANTATION
- ULSTER PLANTATION
- AREA LEFT TO IRISH UNDER CROMWELL'S PL.
- MILE-WIDE STRIP

The plantations in Ireland

C. *The London Guilds*

1. The county of Coleraine was given to The Honourable, The Irish Society, a group of London guilds.
2. The Society built the city of Londonderry and individual guilds built towns such as Draperstown and Salterstown.
3. The guilds were interested only in quick profits and, in spite of their contracts with the government, they took Irish tenants and allowed Irish people to settle in the towns.
4. The guilds abused their contracts so much that Lord Deputy Wentworth fined them heavily and confiscated much of their property.

D. The Towns

1. The planters built many towns. Most were located on good defensive sites and were surrounded by walls. Four streets led from the gates to a central square or diamond where markets were held and the Protestant church and town hall were erected.

2. Most towns had a royal charter which allowed their citizens to elect a town council, usually of twelve burgesses. The burgesses elected the town's provost (mayor) and its members of parliament.

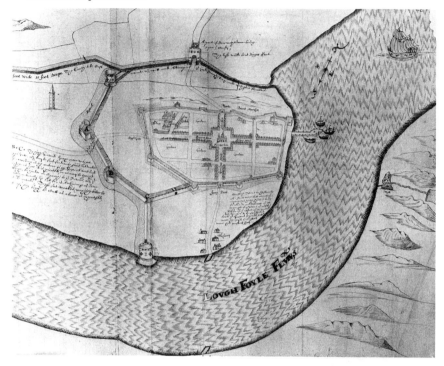

Plan of Derry City. Note the protecting walls, the regular layout and the central square

E. Success?

By 1618 there were 40,000 English and Scottish planters in Ulster and the province was covered with their farms and towns. It seemed as if the plantation were a great success.

THE FINAL PLANTATIONS

A. Rebellion 1641–1650

1. However, many dispossessed land-owners still lived in Ulster. They rebelled in 1641, massacred many planters and destroyed their farms and towns.

2. The Ulster uprising led to a country-wide rebellion which was finally defeated in 1650 by Oliver Cromwell and his English army.

B. The Cromwellian Plantation

1. Cromwell now proposed to plant the entire island with English settlers.
2. All those who had fought against England during the years 1641 and 1650 lost their lands and 'innocent' Irish land-owners were transplanted to Connacht, where they were supposed to receive land equivalent to their former estates. A mile-wide strip along the coast and Shannon was kept for soldiers.
3. The descendants of the Ulster planters were restored to their estates.
4. Land in Munster and Leinster went to pay English soldiers and adventurers (Englishmen who had lent money to pay Cromwell's army).

C. Success?

1. However, many soldiers did not wish to become farmers in Ireland. They sold their land to officers or adventurers and returned to England.
2. Many of those who remained married Irish women and their descendants were no different from their Irish neighbours.
3. Thus Cromwell's attempt to Anglicise Ireland failed.
4. However, he destroyed most of the old Gaelic and Anglo-Norman landlord class and replaced it with one that was English and Protestant.

D. The War of the Two Kings (1688–1692)

1. The remaining Gaelic and Anglo-Norman land-owners fought for James II in his unsuccessful war with William of Orange.
2. Many emigrated after the Treaty of Limerick. William confiscated their lands and gave them to his supporters, thus reinforcing Cromwell's plantation.

E. The Results of Plantation

1. The Gaelic Irish and Anglo-Norman land-owning classes were wiped out.
2. They were replaced by Protestant, English land-owners.
3. However, the Irish labourers were not disturbed but continued to work for their new masters as they had worked for their old ones.
4. Some landlords looked after their estates, their tenants and their labourers. They built towns and fine houses and did much to improve the lives of the people, Catholic and Protestant alike.
5. Other landlords had no interest in their estates and many were absentees. They left their lands undeveloped and exploited their tenants to the limit. This led to many acts of terrorism by downtrodden tenants and labourers during the eighteenth and nineteenth centuries.
6. This new landlord class remained in power until the late nineteenth century when the land acts broke up their estates.

THE AMERICAN REVOLUTION

A. The Thirteen Colonies
1. During the sixteenth and seventeenth centuries, the British set up thirteen colonies in North America.
2. The colonies ruled themselves, usually through elected councils, and the British rarely interfered with them.

B. Tensions
During the 1760s and 1770s, however, tensions developed between Britain and the colonies.
1. The British tried to make the colonists pay taxes to support the army. The colonists claimed that the British had no right to tax them without their consent.
2. British troops 'massacred' five Bostonians during a riot in 1770. *Boston massacre*
3. Navigation Acts passed by the British parliament benefited British trade at the expense of the colonists.
4. In 1773 the British attempted to end widespread smuggling – resulting from (3) – by allowing the British East India Company to sell tea cheaply in the colonies.
5. This led to the Boston Tea Party when Bostonians, dressed as Indians, threw the tea into the harbour.
6. The British retaliated by closing Boston harbour, thus destroying the city's trade.
7. The British also appointed officials to administer the colonies instead of their own elected councils.

C. The First Continental Congress
1. In 1774 delegates from twelve colonies met at Philadelphia.
2. (i) They demanded an end to taxation levied without their consent. (ii) They called for the restoration of the colonies' elected councils and (iii) ordered a boycott of British goods.
3. Some delegates demanded complete independence.

D. War
1. In April 1775 British troops marched on Concord to seize an arms dump. Colonists attacked them at Lexington and killed and wounded many of them.
2. The colonists then besieged Boston.
3. In May the Second Continental Congress appointed George Washington to command an army to defend the rights of the colonists.

1. CONCORD
2. LEXINGTON
3. BUNKER HILL
4. SARATOGA
5. YORKTOWN

▓ 13 COLONIES

The American War of Independence

4. In June the colonists defeated the British at Bunker Hill.
5. The British flooded the colonies with soldiers. Many were German mercenaries, whose brutality added to the resentment felt towards Britain.
6. Thomas Paine's pamphlet *Common Sense* persuaded many more colonists that America should be independent.
7. On 4 July 1776 the Continental Congress finally proclaimed the colonies' independence in the Declaration of Independence.
8. The Americans won a major victory at Saratoga in 1777 and France, Spain and the Netherlands declared war on Britain. Their fleets cut British communications with America and French troops gave the Americans considerable help.
9. The British were finally defeated at Yorktown in 1781 and in 1783 they signed the Treaty of Paris recognising American independence.

E. The Constitution

1. Some Americans wanted each colony to become an independent country but in 1788 the majority accepted a Constitution (a set of basic laws) which set up a federal republic, the United States of America.
2. Each state looks after its own internal affairs.

3. Each state sends two senators and several representatives to Congress to make laws for the country as a whole.
4. Citizens elect the president, who (i) enforces the laws, (ii) commands the armed forces and (iii) appoints the judges of the Supreme Court.
5. The Supreme Court explains the laws and the Constitution.
6. Amendments to the Constitution guarantee to all citizens civil rights such as freedom of speech, religion, assembly and the right to carry weapons.

F. The Importance of the American Revolution
1. A new country was created, a country which is now the most powerful in the world.
2. Ordinary people in many countries realised that it was possible to overthrow tyrannical rulers.
3. This led to revolutions in France, South America and Ireland.
4. The US Constitution has been copied in many countries.

The surrender of General Cornwallis to Washington at Yorktown

THE ANCIEN RÉGIME

A. The Ancien Régime
1. The period c. 1650–1790 in European history is sometimes called the *Ancien Régime* or the Age of Absolutism. These phrases refer to the fact that Europe was ruled by monarchs who had absolute (complete) power over their peoples.
2. Many absolute monarchs were also 'enlightened', i.e. they tried to act for the good of their peoples. Such monarchs included Catherine the Great and Joseph II. However, they never consulted their people because they believed that they knew best.

B. The Philosophes

These enlightened monarchs often followed the ideas of the philosophes, writers who claimed that they were inspired by reason alone. These writers included Montesquieu, Voltaire and Rousseau.

C. Montesquieu (1689–1755)

1. Montesquieu's book *The Persian Letters* was a savage satire on French life and turned many people against the government and the Catholic Church.
2. His book *The Spirit of the Laws* described a form of government which involved the 'separation of powers' among law makers (parliament), law enforcers (government) and interpreters of the law (courts). Montesquieu believed that such a system would prevent tyranny.

D. Voltaire (1693–1778)

Voltaire wrote many plays, novels and essays mocking the nobility of France, the Catholic Church and superstition. His writings led to his (comfortable) imprisonment in the Bastille but they also caused many people to demand changes in the way France was ruled.

E. Rousseau (1712–1778)

Rousseau opened his famous book *The Social Contract* with the lines, 'Man was born free but everywhere he is in chains.' He went on to show how people could be free once more by setting up governments which carried out the 'general will'. Rousseau's writings were very popular among France's middle classes and liberal nobles.

THE FRENCH REVOLUTION (1)

A. France and the American Revolution

The American Revolution affected France in two ways.

1. The Americans' success in defeating George III and in taking control of their own country encouraged many French people to try to win control of France from Louis XVI.
2. Her part in the American War of Independence bankrupt France, and Louis asked the States General (the people's representatives) to help him raise new taxes. However, when they finally met in May 1789 many of the representatives were far more interested in winning control of France than in helping the king.

B. French Society

1. The people of France consisted of three 'estates' (social classes). (i) The first was the clergy. (ii) The second was the nobility. (iii) The third was the common people.

2. The clergy paid no taxes and had their own courts. However, the poor parish priests resented the rich bishops and abbots, most of whom came from noble families.

3. The nobility paid no taxes but controlled all important jobs in the army, courts, civil service and the Church.

4. The common people were the peasants, craftsmen, the urban working class and the rich bourgeoisie (middle class).

5. (i) These people paid many taxes to the government and to the Church. (ii) They had to buy salt from the government (gabelle). (iii) They had to work without wages on the roads (corvée) and (iv) they had to submit to the feudal 'rights' of the local nobles. (v) They had no influence over the government and (vi) they could not get well-paid jobs in the Church, army, courts or civil service.

6. As a result, the Third Estate deeply resented the government and the nobility who exploited them. Many ordinary priests and some nobles supported the Third Estate.

C. The National Assembly

1. This resentment came to a head when the States General met in May 1789.

2. The representatives of the Third Estate and their supporters among the nobility and clergy declared themselves the National Assembly and swore not to disperse until they had given France a Constitution (June 1789).

3. As a result the National Assembly was sometimes called the Constituent Assembly.

D. The Fall of the Ancien Régime

1. Louis XVI was a friendly, brave but rather stupid man. At first he was inclined to let the National Assembly have its way but then his wife, Marie Antoinette, and the great nobles persuaded him to use the army to break up the National Assembly and to take control of the country once again.

2. The people of Paris supported the National Assembly and they feared that Louis would use his troops against them. On 14 July they (i) rioted, (ii) captured a royal fortress, the Bastille, (iii) took over the city government and (iv) set up the National Guard to defend themselves against the king and to keep order in the city.

3. There were similar outbreaks throughout France as (i) the bourgeoisie took over the towns, (ii) the peasants burned the châteaux of unpopular nobles and (iii) army units mutinied.

4. To calm the situation, the National Assembly ended the privileges of the nobles and clergy and issued the 'Declaration of the Rights of Man and of the Citizen', which guaranteed (i) freedom of speech, (ii) freedom of religion, (iii) freedom to own property, (iv) equality before the law and (v) the right to resist tyranny (August 1789).

The storming of the Bastille

5. In October food shortages caused fresh rioting in Paris. A huge mob of women marched to Versailles and forced the king and the National Assembly to return to Paris with them.
6. Louis' power was destroyed and the National Assembly was safe.

THE FRENCH REVOLUTION (2)

A. Work of the National (Constituent) Assembly

Between 1789 and 1791 the National (Constituent) Assembly (i) changed the way the country was administered, (ii) reduced the powers of the king and (iii) took control of the Church.

B. Administration

1. France was divided into departments and communes, areas approximately equal in size and population.
2. Assemblies elected by the citizens controlled each commune and department. These citizens also elected the local judges and formed the local National Guard.
3. France therefore became a country in which the central government had very little authority.

C. The Powers of the King

1. The king lost his right to make laws.
2. However, he could still veto laws passed by the National Assembly.
3. He also appointed the government ministers.

D. The Civil Constitution of the Clergy

1. The National Assembly reorganised the Catholic Church in the Civil Constitution of the Clergy. (i) It confiscated Church land and sold it to raise funds for the government. (ii) It suppressed religious orders and (iii) allowed citizens to elect their bishops and priests.
2. Pope Pius VI condemned the Civil Constitution of the Clergy. Most clergy accepted the pope's condemnation.
3. The National Assembly ordered all non-juring clergy (those who opposed the Civil Constitution) to leave France and persecuted those who remained as enemies of the Revolution.
4. This conflict between supporters of the Church and supporters of the Revolution led to vicious civil wars.

E. The Flight to Varennes

1. Louis was now anxious to regain his authority. He was a devout Catholic and disliked the Civil Constitution of the Clergy. He therefore decided to overthrow the National Assembly and to restore the old system of government.
2. On 21–22 June 1791 the royal family tried to escape to loyal troops in eastern France. However, they were captured at Varennes and sent back to Paris.
3. It was now clear to all that Louis was an enemy of the Revolution.

THE FRENCH REVOLUTION (3)

A. The Legislative Assembly

The Legislative Assembly replaced the National Assembly (1 October 1791). This Assembly contained many who wanted to overthrow Louis, set up a republic and spread democratic ideas throughout Europe.

B. War

1. Many European rulers were worried that events in France would encourage their people to rebel.
2. The rulers of Prussia and Austria now declared that they were ready to restore Louis to his former authority.
3. This annoyed the Legislative Assembly, which declared war on Austria (20 April 1792).

C. The Fall of the Monarchy

1. The war went badly for the French. Austrian and Prussian forces invaded France. People blamed Louis. On 10 August 1792 republican mobs stormed the royal palace and the Legislative Assembly imprisoned Louis.

2. The Legislative Assembly dissolved itself and a new assembly, the Convention, replaced it.
3. On 20 September the French defeated the Austrians and Prussians at Valmy.
4. The Convention (i) abolished the monarchy, (ii) declared a republic, (iii) found Louis guilty of treason and (iv) had him guillotined on 21 January 1793.

The execution of Louis XVI

THE FRENCH REVOLUTION (4)

A. The War Widens

The Convention believed that its armies and ideas of Liberty, Equality and Fraternity could not be beaten. It declared war on many of Europe's monarchs and its enthusiastic republican soldiers won many victories.

B. The Reign of Terror

1. However, many French people disliked the wars, the execution of the king and the persecution of the Church.
2. There were many rebellions against the Convention, which then set up the Committee of Public Safety to deal with the crisis (6 April 1793).
3. The Committee directed a Reign of Terror against all those suspected of opposing the Revolution. Thousands (including many members of the Convention) were guillotined and revolutionary armies devastated the regions that had rebelled.
4. Maximilien Robespierre was the best-known member of the Committee of Public Safety and many people thought that he was personally responsible for the Terror.
5. Early in 1794, it was clear that the Revolution was safe and that the time had come to

end the Terror. However, it seemed as if Robespierre wanted to continue it indefinitely.
6. The Convention turned against him and he was guillotined on 28 July 1794.

C. Enter Napoleon Bonaparte
1. The Convention set up yet another system of government (the Directory) which would keep two-thirds of its members in power.
2. Many people, republicans and royalists alike, resented this and on 5 October 1795 they tried to overthrow the Directory.
3. A young officer, Napoleon Bonaparte, scattered the mobs with a 'whiff of grapeshot' and saved the Directory.

D. The Revolution Comes Full Circle
1. Napoleon Bonaparte was born on Corsica in 1769.
2. He became an officer in the royal artillery but supported the Revolution when it broke out.
3. He was a brilliant general. He won many victories in the revolutionary wars and became France's most popular soldier.
4. In 1804 he proclaimed himself 'emperor of the French' with absolute powers. During the years that followed, he exercised this power more fully than any king had ever exercised power in the history of France. The Revolution had come full circle.

EIGHTEENTH-CENTURY IRELAND

A. The Protestant Ascendancy
1. Following the victory of William of Orange over James II, power in Ireland passed to aristocratic land-owners usually called the Protestant Ascendancy.
2. This Ascendancy feared the country's Catholic majority and parliament enacted the Penal Laws to keep Catholics powerless.

B. The Penal Laws
1. Catholic bishops were outlawed.
2. Parish clergy were ordered to register with the government.
3. Catholics were forbidden to open schools or travel abroad for education.
4. Catholic land-owners had to divide their estates among all their heirs.
5. Catholics were not allowed to own guns.
6. Catholics were forbidden to vote, to join the army or to take a university degree.
7. Many Catholic land-owners became Protestants to keep their estates intact. Those who did not were often forced to sell out to their Protestant neighbours. Thus the

amount of land owned by Irish Catholics decreased rapidly during the eighteenth century.

C. Limitations

1. However, the Protestant Ascendancy did not have complete power because the authority of its parliament was limited by Poynings' Law and the Sixth of George I.
2. Poynings' Law forbade parliament to pass any law which had not previously been approved by the king and his council.
3. The Sixth of George I allowed the British parliament to make laws for Ireland.
4. Some of the Ascendancy resented these laws while merchants and industrialists resented the way the British discriminated against Irish trade and industry.

D. The Volunteers

1. The British sent all their Irish troops to fight the Americans during the War of Independence.
2. Groups of Protestants formed corps of Volunteers to defend the country against invasion. They united under the earl of Charlemont in an army 80,000 strong.

E. Free Trade and 'Independence'

1. Many Volunteers were merchants or industrialists who had suffered because of British trade laws.
2. Because the British were in such trouble in America, the Volunteers were able to use the threat of force to compel them to grant free trade (1779) and to pass the Renunciation Act (1783) which repealed Poynings' Law and the Sixth of George I and granted the Irish parliament 'legislative independence'.
3. Many Penal Laws were repealed so that Catholics would not be tempted to rebel.
4. The Volunteers broke up when the American war ended and the threat of invasion had passed.

F. Corruption

1. However, the British were still able to control the corrupt Irish parliament, though some politicians such as Henry Grattan tried to reform it.
2. The king still appointed the lord lieutenant and chief secretary, who took their orders from the British and not the Irish parliament.
3. Most MPs were easily bribed to pass laws favourable to Britain.

THE UNITED IRISHMEN

A. The Impact of the French Revolution

1. The French Revolution encouraged liberal Protestants like Wolfe Tone to demand a total reform of parliament.
2. In his pamphlet *An Argument on behalf of the Catholics of Ireland*, he stated that parliament could be reformed only if Catholics, Protestants and Dissenters (Presbyterians) forgot their differences and worked together as Irish people.
3. Tone contacted the Society of United Irishmen, a group of Belfast Protestants who had similar ideas, and he founded a branch of the Society in Dublin.

Wolfe Tone

B. The United Irishmen Outlawed

1. By 1795 it was clear that the Irish parliament would not reform itself and many United Irishmen felt that they would have to use force to achieve their aims.
2. Tone sought help from France and the government outlawed the United Irishmen.
3. The United Irishmen continued to recruit new members and led by Edward Fitzgerald they prepared to rebel.

C. Bantry Bay

A French fleet sailed into Bantry Bay in December 1796. Tone was one of its officers. Storms prevented a landing and the fleet had to return to France.

1798

A. Government Terror

1. The government was badly frightened by the attempted French invasion and set about breaking the United Irishmen.
2. (i) The army brutally disarmed the people of Ulster. (ii) Spies kept the government

The Rebellion of 1798

informed on the United Irishmen. (iii) In March 1798 the government arrested many
of the Society's leaders.

B. The Leinster Rebellion

1. Though left without leaders or weapons, the United Irishmen in Leinster rose in
    rebellion (23 May 1798).
2. Government troops defeated them easily at Tara, Carlow and the Curragh.

C. The Wexford Rebellion

1. There were few United Irishmen in Wexford.
2. Nevertheless, the military treated the people very brutally and in sheer desperation
    they rebelled (26 May).
3. The rebels defeated the army at Oulart, Enniscorthy and Wexford but their attempts
    to break out of the county and to spread the rebellion were defeated at Newtownbarry,
    New Ross and Arklow.
4. The rebels were finally beaten at Vinegar Hill (21 June).
5. Their leaders, Bagenal Harvey and John Murphy, were executed, as were thousands of
    ordinary rebels. Many more were transported to Australia or sold as slaves to the king
    of Prussia.

D. The Ulster Rebellion

1. The United Irishmen in Ulster also rebelled in June.
2. Their forces, commanded by Henry Joy McCracken and Henry Monroe, were defeated at Antrim town and Ballinahinch.
3. Their leaders and many ordinary rebels were executed.

E. Humbert's Expedition

1. A small French expedition commanded by General Humbert landed at Killala (22 August 1798).
2. Together with some local allies, the French defeated government troops at the 'Races of Castlebar'.
3. Humbert advanced on Dublin but was defeated at Ballinamuck (8 September).
4. The French prisoners were well treated but their Irish comrades were massacred.

F. The Death of Wolfe Tone

Admiral Bompart, accompanied by Wolfe Tone, tried to land another French force at Lough Swilly in October 1798. They were defeated. Tone was captured. He was sentenced to death but cut his throat and died (19 November).

G. The Act of Union

1. Although the 1798 rebellion had been suppressed by Irish troops in the service of the Irish parliament, William Pitt, the British prime minister, feared that this parliament would be unable to control the country much longer.
2. He therefore decided to control Ireland directly by creating a single United Kingdom of Great Britain and Ireland.
3. He promised Catholics that the remaining Penal Laws would be repealed.
4. He also promised Protestants that they would still enjoy their privileges.
5. He promised Irish merchants that they would prosper under free trade with Britain.
6. He won over the MPs by spending more than one million pounds of (Irish) taxpayers' money in bribes.
7. The Irish parliament voted itself out of existence in 1800 and on 1 January 1801 the United Kingdom of Great Britain and Ireland came into being, with its parliament located at Westminster in London.

11 THE AGRICULTURAL AND INDUSTRIAL REVOLUTIONS

THE AGRICULTURAL REVOLUTION

A. A Population Explosion

The population of Europe increased rapidly in the eighteenth century. This triggered off a demand for more food and more manufactured goods, which brought about the agricultural and industrial revolutions.

B. The Four-Field System

1. Farmers used the three-field system until the eighteenth century. (See p. 44.)
2. During the eighteenth century farmers in Norfolk, especially Viscount 'Turnip' Townsend, pioneered a fourfold system of crop rotation to replace the old three-field system.
3. Wheat, turnips, barley and clover were planted in successive years.

F I E L D

	1	2	3	4
1	WHEAT	TURNIPS	BARLEY	CLOVER
2	CLOVER	WHEAT	TURNIPS	BARLEY
3	BARLEY	CLOVER	WHEAT	TURNIPS
4	TURNIPS	BARLEY	CLOVER	WHEAT

(Y E A R)

FOUR-FIELD ROTATION

4. The turnips and clover made the soil fertile again and provided winter fodder for animals.
5. Thus more arable crops became available and it was no longer necessary to slaughter animals at the beginning of winter.

C. Enclosures

1. Enclosure Acts allowed farmers to consolidate their holdings and to break up the commons in proportion to the size of their farms.

2. Individual farmers now had more land which was easier to cultivate because it formed a single block instead of scattered strips.

3. However, poorer villagers often lost out and had to sell their small holdings to the better-off farmers.

4. They then became farm labourers or emigrated to work in the cities.

D. Other Developments

1. Steam power was not used to work farm machinery until the nineteenth century.

2. However, ploughs were improved and the scythe replaced the sickle in harvesting.

3. (i) Jethro Tull invented a seed drill which set seeds at regular intervals, prevented waste and improved yields. (ii) His horse-hoe was not very successful but (iii) his book *Horse Hoe Husbandry* encouraged farmers to keep their land weed-free and so increased yields.

4. Robert Bakewell developed new ways of breeding cattle and sheep so that larger, meatier animals became available.

5. The educational work of Thomas Coke and Arthur Young did much to spread information about improved agricultural techniques.

THE INDUSTRIAL REVOLUTION: POWER

A. Background

Before the industrial revolution most manufactured goods were made by craftsmen in small workshops using machinery powered by animal, human or water power.

B. Power

1. During the industrial revolution steam power replaced muscle and water power.

2. The earliest steam engines, e.g. those developed by Thomas Savery (1692), were used to pump out mines. They were not very efficient and often exploded.

3. Thomas Newcomen invented a steam engine with condensers and safety valves (1712). This was able to pump out deep mines and it did not explode as often as the earlier engines.

4. James Watt built engines able to change vertical into horizontal movements (1775). These engines were able to power machinery.

THE INDUSTRIAL REVOLUTION: FACTORIES

A. A Great Industry

1. The textile industry had been England's most important industry since the Middle Ages.

Watt's rotative beam engine

2. However, the spinning, cording, weaving and dyeing had been carried out in the home on simple machines powered by workers themselves.
3. These processes were slow. Very little cloth was made and it was very expensive.

B. Inventions

1. John Kay invented the flying shuttle to speed up weaving (1773).
2. James Hargreaves' spinning jenny (1764) and Crompton's mule (1779) speeded up spinning.
3. Edmund Cartwright invented the steam-driven power loom which accelerated weaving (1785).
4. Louis de Berthollet discovered (1785) that chlorine could bleach cloth in a few hours. Previously, sunlight and soda had taken months to carry out the process.

C. Factories

1. Power-driven textile machines were large and expensive. Big buildings were needed to contain them and only a few wealthy industrialists could afford them.
2. Working conditions in the textile factories were horrific. (i) The factories were dark and damp. (ii) Employees worked twelve to fifteen hours a day. (iii) Wages were low and (iv) there were heavy fines for breaking spindles, opening windows, being late . . . (v) The machines were unprotected and workers were often killed and mutilated.
3. (i) Some spinners and weavers continued to work at home. (ii) They became poorer and poorer because they could not compete with the factories. (iii) Many died from hunger and bad living conditions. (iv) Others, nicknamed Luddites, destroyed machinery in the factories and (v) many were executed for their acts of terrorism.

Textile workers. Note the children

D. Iron and Steel

1. In 1700 Britain's iron and steel industry was very backward.
2. It produced only a little, low-quality pig-iron, and high-quality steel had to be imported from Sweden.
3. However, new developments led to a rapid expansion of the industry and to a better-quality product.
4. Abraham Darby discovered how to use coke instead of charcoal to smelt iron ore (1709).
5. His grandson, another Abraham, built England's first iron bridge.
6. Henry Cort developed puddling and rolling to change impure pig-iron into good-quality wrought iron (1784).
7. Henry Bessemer invented a converter which made pig-iron into fine steel at a very low cost (1857).

E. The Mines

1. The new factories required huge amounts of coal to power their machines and the new pumping equipment made it possible for the miners to dig even deeper underground.
2. The living and working conditions of the miners were unspeakable. (i) Cramped conditions, bad air, poisoned gases and rock falls disfigured and crippled them at an early age. (ii) Children were often used to carry coal because their small size allowed them to travel easily through the narrow passages of the mine. (iii) Parliamentary reports tell us that children as young as four were employed underground and (iv) that young girls ruptured their backs carrying loads their fathers were unable to lift.

Child 'hurrier' in a coal mine

THE INDUSTRIAL REVOLUTION: TRANSPORT

A. Roads

1. Until the late 1600s each English parish was responsible for maintaining the roads passing through it. As a result England's roads were notoriously bad.
2. From 1663 the government allowed private companies called turnpike trusts to maintain some roads in return for tolls (fees).

B. Famous Engineers

1. 'Blind Jack' Metcalf, Thomas Telford and John Macadam were famous engineers involved in turnpiking.
2. They built roads with tightly packed gravel and stones laid on firm foundations of heavy rocks.
3. These improved roads greatly speeded up travel by stage-coach.
4. However, the stage-coaches were slow, uncomfortable and expensive and only the rich could afford to use them.

C. Canals

1. Where possible, heavy goods were moved on river barges.
2. To make this movement easier, rivers were widened and deepened.
3. The Newry Canal was the first purpose-built canal in the British Isles (1741).
4. (i) In Britain James Brindley built the Bridgewater Canal linking the coalfields at Warsley with Manchester (1761). (ii) This was a remarkable work of engineering, especially as Brindley had no formal training and was almost illiterate.
5. The Bridgewater Canal was very profitable. 'Canal fever' gripped speculators throughout Britain and by the end of the century all the great ports and rivers were linked by canals.
6. However, the canals were soon ousted by the railways.

D. The Railways

1. James Watt, Richard Trevithick and William Hedley tried to use steam power to move wagons along iron rails. However, George Stephenson was probably the most famous of the early railway engineers.
2. (i) He started life as an illiterate herdsman but (ii) went to work at a colliery. (iii) He built his first locomotive, 'Blucher', in 1814. (iv) In 1825 he built the Stockton and Darlington railway with his locomotive the 'Rocket' pulling its passenger wagons.
3. His Liverpool–Manchester railway (1830) proved very profitable and railway mania swept Britain. By 1870 there were 22,000 km of railway linking the country's main towns.

E. Steamships

1. Steam was used to power ships even before it was used to power railway locomotives.
2. William Symington built a steam-powered boat to tow barges on the Clyde Canal (1802).
3. In 1812 the *Savannah* crossed the Atlantic powered by sails and steam-driven paddles.
4. The *Great Britain* was the first propeller-driven ship. It first crossed the Atlantic in 1843.

F. Importance of the New Transport Systems

1. Goods could now be transported more quickly and more cheaply than ever before.
2. This reduced prices, stimulated demand and speeded up the industrial revolution.
3. The iron and steel industry expanded to fill the demand for trains, tracks and iron ships.
4. In 1840 Thomas Cooke organised the first ever day-trip and so began the modern tourist industry.

INDUSTRIAL SOCIETY

A. Slums

1. The factories enticed many poor people into the towns for work and drove many wealthy people into the more pleasant countryside.
2. Many large town houses were subdivided into tiny apartments and let to the workers at a high rent.
3. Many employers built long terraces of 'back-to-back' houses and accommodated their workers in them, a family per room.
4. These houses had no toilets or running water and the people had to use street-side water pumps and public latrines.

A London slum

B. Disease

1. These slums had no proper sewers. Their refuse was not collected. All waste was dumped into the streets and yards where it decayed and became the home of vermin.
2. Drinking water was often contaminated by waste from the public toilets.
3. Fresh food was rarely eaten but people drank large amounts of alcohol. Disease was widespread and outbreaks of cholera occurred regularly.
4. The British government encouraged local councils to improve housing and health throughout the nineteenth century but the Board of Health did not have power to enforce proper sanitary regulations until 1875.

C. The Factory Acts

1. A lot of MPs were distressed by the bad conditions endured by many factory workers and miners, especially women and children.
2. Other MPs had become rich because of these very conditions and they were reluctant to change them.
3. Nevertheless, MPs such as Lord Salisbury persuaded parliament to pass mine and factory acts. These (i) regulated hours of work and safety conditions, (ii) appointed government inspectors to see that regulations were carried out, and finally (iii) forbade the employment of women and children in mines.
4. Eventually the employment of children was forbidden altogether.

D. Trade Unions

1. In 1800, during the Napoleonic Wars, the British government banned trade unions as revolutionary.
2. The ban ended in 1825 but strikes remained illegal.

3. It was also possible to use other laws against trade unionists. In 1834 the 'Tolpuddle Martyrs', who tried to form a trade union, were transported to Australia for taking illegal oaths.

4. In 1833 Robert Owen organised the Grand National Consolidated Trade Union. However, it was badly organised and broke up in 1835.

5. The Amalgamated Society of Engineers was founded in 1851. Its members were well paid. They were able to fund their union properly and to negotiate with their employers from a position of strength. The union looked after sick or unemployed members and it became a model for many unions formed by skilled workers during the 1860s.

6. Unskilled workers were too poor to form large general unions until the 1880s.

7. A strike by London match-girls in 1888 encouraged the growth of these unions.

8. (i) In 1889 Ben Tillet led the Dockers' Union in a strike for a 'tanner [2·5p] an hour'. (ii) They were supported by other unions and by Cardinal Manning of Westminster and (iii) their employers granted their demands after a month's strike.

9. (i) The unions suffered a set-back in 1901 when the courts declared that trade unionists had to compensate their employers for losses suffered during a strike (Taff Vale case). (ii) The Trades Disputes Act 1906 declared that unions were no longer responsible for such losses. The strike weapon and the unions were saved.

E. Chartism

1. Many reformers believed that England's workers would never win decent living conditions until they had political power.

2. William Lovett drew up the 'People's Charter' which called for: (i) the vote for all adult males; (ii) secret voting; (iii) constituencies with equal populations; (iv) an end to property qualifications for MPs; (v) wages for MPs; (vi) annual general elections.

3. Three mass petitions were presented to parliament demanding the enactment of the Charter. Parliament refused and the Chartist movement collapsed. However, the first five demands were granted by 1918.

F. Robert Owen

1. Robert Owen was probably the most important individual working for the rights of workers.

2. He was a brilliant businessman and he owned a large cotton mill at New Lanark employing 2,000 workers.

3. He (i) paid his employees high wages, (ii) provided them with good housing and schools and (iii) set up shops where they could buy cheap clothes and food.

4. He was involved in (i) the Grand National Consolidated Trade Union and (ii) the Cooperative movement.

5. His book A New View of Society proposed that self-sufficient cooperative villages

should be established throughout the country, where the people would work for the common good. However, all his efforts to build such villages, e.g. New Harmony in the USA, failed.

IRELAND c. 1850

A. Dublin
1. Dublin was the second most important city of the empire, though many English cities outstripped it in size during the nineteenth century.
2. It had few great industries. Its skilled craftsmen worked in small workshops. Its unskilled workers were labourers or porters and were frequently unemployed.
3. The Liberties were the oldest part of Dublin and many of its buildings were terrible slums.
4. Some fine squares and streets had been laid out at the end of the eighteenth century (Georgian Dublin). However, much of this area fell into decay when aristocrats and politicians emigrated to London after the Union (1801).
5. There were no huge developments of workers' houses like those common in English cities.

B. Belfast
1. Unlike Dublin, Belfast developed as an industrial city during the nineteenth century.
2. Its industries were ship-building, engineering and textile-making.
3. Many country people came into Belfast to work in the factories and many Scots came to work in the metal industries.
4. These people were accommodated in long terraces of workers' houses similar to those frequently found in English cities.
5. Sectarian rioting was very common.

C. Country Towns
1. Country towns were generally ill kept.
2. They had few industries. These were mainly brewing, distilling, milling or craftwork.
3. Towns were primarily service centres for the surrounding countryside, and fairs and markets were very important.

D. Landlords
1. Wealthy noblemen lived in splendid mansions (e.g. Carton House) but these were exceptional.
2. Most big houses were much less magnificent.
3. Many landlords were more interested in sport or gambling than in developing their estates.
4. There were, however, landlords, e.g. the Pakenhams, who worked hard to improve their properties.

5.   Many land-owners became absentees after the Union and they appointed agents to run their estates.

E. The Farmers and Cottiers

1.   Most estates were divided into large farms which were usually let on long leases.
2.   Farmers frequently subdivided their farms among their children or sublet small farms to cottiers who paid for their land with their labour.
3.   The wealthy farmers grew wheat or kept cattle and often lived in large comfortable houses.
4.   The cottiers lived in tiny mud-walled cottages and grew potatoes on their tiny plots.
5.   In some parts of the country, the cottiers lived in sod cabins or in huts made from beach boulders or even in bog-holes!

F. The Great Famine

1.   The potato provided the staple diet for the poor.
2.   It was easy to grow, it was abundant and it was nutritious.
3.   The people sometimes ate salted fish or bacon but rarely had fresh meat.
4.   Blight struck the potato crop between 1845 and 1848 and about one million died from starvation or diseases associated with malnutrition.
5.   The government and private charities, e.g. organised by Quakers, were unable to cope with the problem.
6.   The cottier class was wiped out in many parts of the country and the old habit of subdividing holdings stopped: it threatened starvation.
7.   Instead, farmers began to consolidate their holdings.
8.   Fewer people married and those who did married later in life.
9.   Many emigrated, thus beginning a trend that continues to this day, and Ireland's population, which had been rising quickly since the 1700s, went into a decline from which it has never recovered.

G. Violence

1.   The rapidly growing population between 1700 and 1840 led to a great demand for land and to high rents.
2.   This caused great bitterness between people bidding for the same land, between landlord and tenant, and between tenants and 'grabbers' offering higher rents in order to displace them.
3.   Tenants often formed secret societies to terrorise landlords or land-grabbers.
4.   In Ulster religious differences caused much violence between Protestant secret societies, e.g. Orangemen, and Catholic ones, e.g. Defenders.
5.   Fights between factions, e.g. the Shanavests and the Black Mulvihills, occurred regularly at fairs though nobody knew why. People were sometimes killed during these fights.
6.   The Irish Constabulary established in 1836 did much to end this violence.

12 POLITICAL DEVELOPMENTS IN IRELAND C.1886-1923

THE NINETEENTH CENTURY

A. The Act of Union
1. The Act of Union creating the United Kingdom of Great Britain and Ireland came into force on 1 January 1801.
2. In parliament, which met at Westminster, British MPs heavily outnumbered Irish ones.
3. They neglected Irish problems and many nationalists believed that the situation would improve only when Ireland gained some independence.

B. The Republican Tradition
1. Some nationalists wanted to set up an independent republic by force.
2. Robert Emmet, the Young Irelanders and the Fenians rebelled in 1803, 1848 and 1867.
3. These rebellions were easily defeated but the republican tradition lived on in the Irish Republican Brotherhood (IRB).

C. The Constitutional Tradition
1. Few nationalists desired total independence; most wanted some links with Britain.
2. These moderate nationalists tried to achieve their aims constitutionally (peacefully) but parliament refused to change the Act of Union in any way.

THE HOME RULE MOVEMENT

A. Home Rule
1. Isaac Butt set up the Home Rule movement in 1870.
2. Home Rulers wanted an Irish parliament to control the country's internal affairs, leaving Westminster to control foreign affairs, the army, the economy, etc.
3. Home Rule became very popular in Ireland and shortly after C.S. Parnell became leader of the movement (1880), most Irish MPs were Home Rulers.

B. The First Home Rule Bill
1. Parnell persuaded the Liberal prime minister, W.E. Gladstone, that Ireland should be given Home Rule.
2. However, parliament rejected his first Home Rule Bill (1886).

C. S. Parnell

C. The Fall of Parnell

1. In 1890 W. O'Shea divorced his wife because of her adultery with Parnell.
2. Most Home Rule MPs demanded that Parnell resign to avoid discrediting the movement.
3. Parnell refused. The party split between a minority who supported Parnell and a majority who opposed him.
4. Parnell died (1891).
5. The party reunited under John Redmond (1899).

D. The Second Home Rule Bill

1. Gladstone persuaded the House of Commons to accept his second Home Rule Bill (1893).
2. However, the House of Lords rejected it.
3. Gladstone resigned and the Conservatives won the general election which followed.

KILLING HOME RULE BY KINDNESS

A. Conservative Policies

1. The Conservatives decided 'to kill Home Rule by kindness', i.e. to introduce badly needed changes into Ireland and so make the people happy with the Act of Union.
2. These changes involved (i) land, (ii) economic and (iii) local government reform.

B. Land Reform

1. Irish tenant farmers paid very high rents throughout most of the nineteenth century.
2. After 1870 the Land League and the Home Rulers pressured Liberal governments into passing reforming land acts.
3. The Conservative government now enacted laws which provided loans to farmers to buy out their land and by the early 1900s most Irish farmers owned their farms.

C. Economic Reform

1. The Conservative government set up the Congested Districts' Board (CDB) to develop remote west coast areas.
2. The CDB (i) developed fishing; (ii) reclaimed land; (iii) set up cottage industries; (iv) built roads and railways; (v) improved housing and (vi) subsidised emigration.

D. Local Government Reform

1. The Local Government Act (1898) set up county and district councils.
2. These enabled people to run their own areas and the Conservatives hoped that this would satisfy the demand for Home Rule.
3. This did not happen. Instead these councils supported the Dáil during the War of Independence and so helped to end British rule.

IRISH-IRELAND

A. West Britain

1. At the end of the nineteenth century it seemed that many Irish people were becoming 'West Britons', uninterested in Irish sports, language or culture and copying English music, sport and fashions.
2. Some nationalists disliked this trend and tried to interest people in an 'Irish-Ireland'.

B. The GAA

1. The Gaelic Athletic Association (GAA) was founded by Michael Cusack in 1884.
2. The GAA aimed to develop nationalism in its members through their taking part in Irish sports.
3. It (i) laid down rules for its games, (ii) organised many competitions and so (iii) made people proud of their local areas and country.
4. However, the GAA 'banned' soldiers, policemen and those who played 'foreign' games. This ban led to bad feeling in many communities.

C. Decline of Irish

The Irish language declined rapidly during the nineteenth century.

1. There was massive emigration of Irish-speaking people.
2. The Catholic Church and the national schools emphasised that English was the language of progress and prosperity.
3. Many people regarded Irish as a sign of backwardness.

D. The Gaelic League

1. In 1893 Douglas Hyde, Eoin MacNeill and Eoin O'Growney founded the Gaelic League (i) to halt the decline of Irish; (ii) to restore Irish to where it had been spoken

and (iii) to create a modern literature in Irish.

2. The League (i) trained language teachers and (ii) set up clubs where people could learn Irish. (iii) It produced books and newspapers in Irish and (iv) encouraged Irish culture through local (feiseanna) and national (oireachtais) festivals.

3. The League was very successful. (i) It slowed the decline of Irish and (ii) its clubs were some of the few places where all groups within Irish society met on equal terms.

4. However, the IRB used the League to recruit new members.

5. Hyde, the president of the League, objected but he was forced to resign. Many Protestants and unionists followed him and the League ceased to be a unifying element in Irish life.

E. The Anglo-Irish Literary Movement

1. Writers such as Lady Gregory, W.B. Yeats and J.M. Synge could not speak Irish.

2. They tried to create an Irish literature in English (i) by writing about Irish themes and (ii) by using the kind of English spoken in Ireland.

3. Many of their plays staged in the Abbey Theatre were very popular.

4. Some plays, e.g. *The Countess Cathleen*, were very political and encouraged people to join extreme nationalist movements.

5. Other plays, e.g. *The Playboy of the Western World*, were unpopular because they seemed to mock the Irish people.

F. Sinn Féin

1. Arthur Griffith set out his ideas in a book, *The Resurrection of Hungary*, and in his newspaper *Sinn Féin*.

2. Griffith believed that Home Rule did not give Ireland enough independence and he claimed that the methods of the Home Rulers had failed.

3. Griffith wanted Irish MPs to stay away from Westminster, and to set up a parliament in Dublin which the Irish people would obey. This would force the British to establish

Arthur Griffith

a Dual Monarchy, i.e. a political system in which Ireland and Britain would be equal and independent but would continue to share the same monarch.

4. Griffith wanted Ireland to be economically self-sufficient. He believed that an Irish parliament should protect Irish industries by taxing imports, thus encouraging Irish people to buy Irish goods.

5. Griffith founded a political party, Sinn Féin (1905). However, he was not a good leader and the party made little progress. Nevertheless, extreme nationalists were often called Sinn Féiners.

G. Importance

1. These Irish-Ireland movements showed people that they were not British.
2. This encouraged many to seek separation from Britain.
3. Some used constitutional methods, e.g. Home Rulers and Sinn Féiners, but others joined the IRB and prepared for armed rebellion.

THE LABOUR MOVEMENT

A. Conditions in Dublin

1. During the 1900s Dublin's unskilled workers were very badly paid. They were frequently unemployed and they lived in very bad conditions.
2. Many suffered from malnutrition and ill health.
3. Employers and landlords were often important members of the Home Rule Party or of Dublin Corporation and therefore workers had nobody to help them.

B. James Larkin and James Connolly

1. In 1909 James Larkin and James Connolly set up the Irish Transport and General Workers' Union (ITGWU).
2. The union organised strikes and forced employers to increase wages.

C. The 1913 Strike and Lock-Out

1. William Martin Murphy organised the employers to fight the ITGWU.
2. In 1913 he sacked employees who belonged to the ITGWU.
3. On 26 August Larkin called a strike in Murphy's businesses.
4. The employers hit back by locking out all their workers whether they were union members or not.
5. The workers and their families suffered greatly during the winter of 1913–14 even though they were helped by British trade unionists and women's organisations led by Countess Markievicz and Hanna Sheehy Skeffington.
6. There were many demonstrations and the police killed several people during baton-charges.

7. Some workers set up the Irish Citizen Army to defend themselves against police brutality.

8. Employers and workers alike lost heavily and both groups were happy to end the conflict early in 1914.

D. The Irish Citizen Army

1. Larkin spent 1914–23 in America and Connolly took charge of the Labour movement and the Citizen Army.

2. He believed that Irish workers would get a fair deal only when they set up a socialist workers' republic.

3. Following the outbreak of World War I he began to plot rebellion.

THE HOME RULE CRISIS 1912–1914

A. The Third Home Rule Bill

1. After the 1910 general election John Redmond's Home Rulers held the 'balance of power' in the House of Commons and neither Liberals nor Conservatives could rule without their support.

2. The Home Rulers agreed to support the Liberals if they introduced a Home Rule Bill.

3. They did. The Bill passed the Commons (1912) but it was defeated in the Lords. The Home Rulers were not worried. The 1911 Parliament Act declared that the Lords could halt a bill approved by the Commons for two years only. Therefore Ireland would have Home Rule in 1914.

4. However, neither the British Conservatives nor the Ulster unionists would accept Home Rule and they set about defeating it using forces outside parliament.

John Redmond

B. Unionist Opposition

Ulster unionists and Protestants opposed Home Rule.

1. They believed that 'Home Rule is Rome Rule', i.e. that a government dominated by Roman Catholics would persecute their religion.

2. They felt that Home Rule would fatally weaken the empire.

3. They feared that their industries would lose their markets if their links with Britain were loosened.

A Unionist propaganda postcard predicting the economic decline of Belfast under Home Rule

C.   Resistance

1. Edward Carson and James Craig led unionist opposition to Home Rule.
2. They set up the Ulster Provisional Government to rule the North if Home Rule became law.
3. On Ulster Day (28 September 1912) one million demonstrators signed the Solemn League and Covenant promising to oppose Home Rule by force if necessary.
4. They organised the Ulster Volunteer Force (UVF), 100,000 strong, for this purpose.
5. The UVF landed a huge consignment of arms at Larne (24 April 1914).
6. British army officers stationed at the Curragh threatened to resign if they were ordered to enforce Home Rule in Ulster.

Edward Carson and James Craig (on his left) signing the Solemn League and Covenant

D. The Irish Volunteers

1. Nationalists were angered by the actions of the unionists.
2. Eoin MacNeill suggested that they should form a volunteer force to defend Home Rule. On 25 November 1913 the Irish Volunteers were formed with MacNeill as chief of staff.

E. The Howth Gun-Running

1. The Irish Volunteers expanded rapidly.
2. On 26 July 1914 they landed rifles at Howth.
3. The army and police tried but failed to capture the weapons and soldiers fired into a jeering crowd at Bachelor's Walk, killing four and wounding thirty-seven people.
4. Nationalists were furious when they contrasted this with the way the government ignored unionist gun-runners.
5. However, the outbreak of World War I and an outpouring of loyalty to the king prevented widespread protests.

F. Partition

1. To prevent war in Ireland Prime Minister Asquith forced Redmond to agree to partition, i.e. to divide the country between Home Rulers and unionists.
2. Home Rulers, unionists and Liberals held many talks but failed to agree on the areas to be partitioned or for how long.
3. In August 1914 the government decided to postpone Home Rule and the question of partition until World War I was over.

THE 1916 RISING

A. The Irish Volunteers Split

1. In September 1914 John Redmond called on the Irish Volunteers to join the British army.
2. Many did, but Eoin MacNeill and the rest refused, declaring that they served Ireland not Britain.

B. The IRB

1. Thomas Clarke and Sean MacDermott took over the IRB (c. 1907).
2. They brought new men into the Brotherhood many of whom became prominent in the Irish Volunteers.
3. In 1914 the IRB decided to take advantage of the world war by staging a rebellion.
4. Their military council began to make plans and sent Roger Casement to Germany to obtain weapons.
5. The IRB knew that Connolly was also plotting rebellion and they persuaded him to join in a rising planned for Easter Sunday 1916.

C. *P.H. Pearse (1879–1916)*

1. Patrick Pearse was an important member of the IRB.
2. He had studied law but he was more interested in education and the Irish language.
3. He ran St Enda's School where he encouraged an Irish atmosphere by emphasising the Irish language and culture. His school was unusual for its wide curriculum and its gentleness.
4. At first Pearse had supported Home Rule but he reacted against unionist violence by becoming an extreme nationalist and joining the IRB and the Volunteers.

P. H. Pearse

D. *Preparations*

1. Pearse became director of operations in the Volunteers and during 1914–16 he had them take part in many military exercises to prepare for the Rising.
2. Few Volunteers realised that they were being used by the IRB or that the manoeuvres planned for Easter Sunday 1916 were to be a full-scale rebellion.

E. *Postponement*

1. On Good Friday the British captured the German ship *Aud* off Kerry with weapons for the rebellion. They also captured Casement, who had landed from a submarine.
2. MacNeill, who opposed rebellion, now became aware of the IRB plot and issued a 'Countermanding Order' cancelling the Easter Sunday manoeuvres. As MacNeill was their commander, the Volunteers obeyed him.
3. However, the IRB decided to stage the Rising in Dublin on Easter Monday, hoping that the country would follow.

F. *Easter Week*

1. On Easter Monday Volunteers and Citizen Army soldiers took over the GPO and other buildings in Dublin and Pearse read the Proclamation of the Republic to a few puzzled onlookers.
2. British troops (many of them Irish) attacked the rebel positions with overwhelming force.

Imaginative drawing of the GPO during Easter Week.
Note Pearse and Clarke on the left and Connolly lying wounded on the stretcher

3. By the end of the week the rebel garrisons were isolated one from another and their headquarters at the GPO was in flames.
4. Connolly and Pearse realised that their position was hopeless and surrendered on Saturday, 29 April 1916.
5. Fighting also took place in Wexford, Galway and Meath.

G. Losses
1. Three hundred people were killed. One thousand were injured.
2. Most were civilians or looters caught in cross-fire.
3. Many important buildings were destroyed and central Dublin was completely wrecked.

1916–1918

A. All Changed
At the end of Easter Week 1916, most Irish people were hostile to the rebels. By 1918, however, the majority regarded them as heroes and wanted Ireland to be an independent republic. This change happened mainly because of British errors of judgment.

B. Errors of Judgment
1. The British imprisoned many people who took no part in the Rising. This caused widespread resentment.
2. Fifteen rebel leaders were executed. All showed great courage and won the admiration of Irish nationalists.

3. The Home Rulers lost support as John Redmond condemned the rebels after they had become popular in Ireland.

4. During 1916–17 Ulster unionists continued to block Home Rule. It was clear that the Home Rulers had no influence with the British and people switched their support to Sinn Féin, the only alternative nationalist political movement.

5. Rebel prisoners released during 1917–18 re-established the Volunteers (now called the Irish Republican Army).

6. The support for Sinn Féin was shown when Eamon de Valera (the senior Volunteer officer to survive the Rising) was elected to parliament (10 July 1917).

7. In 1918 the British tried to enforce conscription in Ireland. Sinn Féin led the successful resistance to the proposal and so became very popular.

C. The 1918 General Election

1. World War I ended on 11 November 1918.
2. A general election took place immediately.
3. The results (below) showed that most people supported Sinn Féin and total independence.

Sinn Féin 73 MPs; Home Rulers 6 MPs; Unionists 26 MPs.

THE INDEPENDENCE STRUGGLE

A. The First Dáil

1. On 7 January 1919 twenty-seven Sinn Féin MPs met in Dublin's Mansion House and set up Dáil Éireann.

2. The Dáil declared the independence of Ireland, set up a government, sent a delegation to the peace talks at Versailles and approved a Democratic Programme.

3. The Democratic Programme drawn up by Thomas Johnson of the Labour Party promised widespread social and economic reforms. Few were carried out.

4. Sean T. O'Kelly led the delegation to Versailles but was not allowed to attend the peace conference.

5. Later, de Valera was elected president of the Dáil. He appointed the following ministers: (i) Michael Collins, finance; (ii) Arthur Griffith, vice-president and home affairs; (iii) Cathal Brugha, defence; (iv) Countess Markievicz, labour; (v) W.T. Cosgrave, local government.

B. De Valera in America

1. De Valera went to the USA (June 1919) to win support for Irish independence.
2. American politicians ignored him but he won massive public and financial support.
3. He was in the USA until December 1920 and to some extent lost track of events in Ireland.

C. The Work of the Dáil

1. It was very difficult for Dáil ministers to do their work. They were on the run from British forces. They had few civil servants. However, some had very important successes.
2. Griffith led the country while de Valera was in America.
3. Collins raised a large public loan to help with the independence struggle.
4. Brugha tried to coordinate the activities of the IRA.
5. Cosgrave and Kevin O'Higgins persuaded the local authorities to support the Dáil. This made it very difficult for the British to govern the country.
6. They also helped to set up the Dáil (Sinn Féin) courts. These took over the administration of justice in many parts of the country and so undermined British authority.

D. The Fighting

1. The IRA did not believe that the British would give in to the Dáil and Sinn Féin without force being used.
2. Volunteers (i) organised boycotts of policemen, (ii) ambushed police patrols, (iii) destroyed police barracks and (iv) formed flying columns to fight the British army.
3. Collins was director of intelligence for the IRA. His spies told him about British activities and his special 'Squad' killed British intelligence agents.

Michael Collins

E. British Response

1. Some RIC men murdered those they suspected of belonging to the IRA or Sinn Féin.
2. The British outlawed the Dáil, Sinn Féin, the IRA, and interned without trial many of their members.
3. Captured IRA soldiers were court-martialled and many were executed.
4. Special forces, the Black and Tans and Auxiliaries, were recruited in England. They fought the IRA and tried to terrorise the people into abandoning the Independence movement.

5.   British forces also carried out official reprisals whenever IRA attacks took place. These often involved destroying the homes of innocent people.

6.   This brutality angered the population and turned them even more fiercely against the British.

F.   Climax

The war climaxed in October/November 1920.

1.   Terence MacSwiney, Lord Mayor of Cork, died after a seventy-two-day hunger-strike.

2.   Eighteen-year-old Kevin Barry was hanged for his part in an ambush.

3.   IRA soldiers held Ballinalee for several days against British forces.

4.   On Bloody Sunday (i) Collins's Squad killed fourteen British spies. (ii) That afternoon British forces killed twelve people in Croke Park. (iii) Three prisoners were later murdered in Dublin Castle.

5.   A British patrol was wiped out at Kilmichael, Co. Cork.

6.   Black and Tans burned the centre of Cork in reprisal.

G.   The Government of Ireland Act 1920

1.   In December 1920 the British parliament tried to solve the Irish problem by passing the Government of Ireland Act. This set up two home-rule-type parliaments, one for Northern Ireland (Antrim, Derry, Down, Fermanagh, Tyrone, Armagh), the other for the remaining twenty-six counties.

2.   Most southerners ignored the Act.

3.   However, northern unionists elected MPs to their parliament, which met in Belfast on 7 June 1921.

TRUCE AND TREATY

A.   In Search of Peace

1.   By mid-1921, both sides wanted peace.

2.   The IRA was exhausted and short of supplies.

3.   The British were embarrassed by their inability to defeat a small guerrilla army.

4.   Many ordinary British people were ashamed of their government's behaviour and pressured their MPs to find a fair solution to the troubles in Ireland.

5.   De Valera was anxious for peace before the country fell into total chaos.

6.   Both sides agreed to a truce (cease-fire) on 11 July 1921.

B.   The Treaty Negotiations

1.   In November 1921 Collins and Griffith led an Irish delegation to London to discuss with the British government a final settlement of the differences between their countries.

2. De Valera refused to go.
3. None of the Irish had any experience in international negotiations.
4. They were at a considerable disadvantage when it came to dealing with people like Lloyd George and Winston Churchill, statesmen with a world reputation.
5. Talks lasted until 6 December 1921 when the Irish accepted the final British offer under threat of 'immediate and terrible war'.

C. The Anglo-Irish Treaty (1921)

1. The twenty-six counties were established as the Irish Free State.
2. The Free State joined the British Commonwealth on the same terms as Canada.
3. All TDs had to take an oath of allegiance to the monarch.
4. The British navy was given bases at Cobh, Berehaven and Lough Swilly.
5. A Boundary Commission was to settle the border between Northern Ireland and the Free State.

D. The Treaty Debates

1. The Dáil discussed the Treaty in a series of bitter debates (December 1921–January 1922).
2. Some TDs rejected the Treaty because: (i) it did not give Ireland total independence; (ii) they could not take the oath of allegiance; (iii) they objected to the Treaty ports and (iv) they did not like partition.
3. Other TDs accepted the Treaty because: (i) it brought peace; (ii) it was the best deal possible; (iii) it gave the country a great amount of freedom and (iv) it gave Ireland the chance to obtain even more independence by peaceful means.
4. The Treaty was accepted on 7 January 1922 by sixty-four votes to fifty-seven.

THE CIVIL WAR

A. Origins

1. De Valera now resigned as president of the Dáil.
2. Griffith replaced him and Collins took charge of the change-over from British to Irish rule.
3. Anti-Treaty IRA units occupied barracks as British forces left.
4. Pro-Treaty IRA units formed the National Army under Collins.
5. In Dublin Rory O'Connor's Anti-Treaty forces occupied the Four Courts, sniped at Collins's troops and kidnapped one of his senior officers.
6. Collins then borrowed artillery from the British and attacked the Four Courts (27 June 1922).

B. The Fighting

1. The Four Courts were quickly captured.
2. The National Army speedily overran IRA positions throughout the country.
3. The IRA then conducted a guerrilla war against the National Army.
4. Griffith died suddenly (12 August 1922) and Collins was killed at Béal na Bláth ten days later.
5. Cosgrave and O'Higgins took charge of the Free State government and Richard Mulcahy took command of the National Army.
6. Both sides carried out atrocities and the Free State government shot seventy-seven IRA prisoners as 'a warning and a reprisal'.
7. Liam Lynch, the IRA chief of staff, was killed (10 April 1923).
8. His successor, Frank Aiken, knew that victory was impossible and he ordered a cease-fire (24 May 1923).

C. Cost

The cost of the Civil War was considerable.

1. Many of the country's most talented leaders were dead (e.g. Collins, Griffith, Lynch, Brugha).
2. Four thousand people had been killed and many more were wounded.
3. Trade and commerce came to a standstill.
4. Roads, railways, bridges and barracks were destroyed.
5. There was widespread lawlessness.
6. A profound hatred developed between those Republicans and Free Staters, a hatred which disfigured Irish public life for many years.

13 PEACE AND WAR IN EUROPE

THE LEGACY OF WORLD WAR I

A. The Great War

1. World War I lasted from August 1914 to November 1918.
2. It was not the longest war ever fought but, until World War II, no war had ever caused so much suffering or so much damage. It was often simply described as 'the Great War' or 'the war to end all wars'.

Europe in 1914

NO = NORWAY
SWE = SWEDEN
D = DENMARK
N = NETHERLANDS
B = BELGIUM
GB = GREAT BRITAIN
IR = IRELAND
SW = SWITZERLAND
R = ROMANIA
BU = BULGARIA
S = SERBIA
M = MONTENEGRO
A = ALBANIA
G = GREECE

B. The Treaty of Versailles

1. The Western Allies (Britain, France, the USA, etc.) defeated the Central Powers (Germany, Austria-Hungary, etc.) and forced them to accept the Treaty of Versailles.
2. Under the Treaty of Versailles the Germans (i) lost territory to France and Poland; (ii) were forced to pay reparations; (iii) had to limit their armed forces and (iv) had to leave the Rhineland demilitarised.
3. The Austro-Hungarian empire was divided into several small states.
4. Most Germans resented the Treaty of Versailles and were determined to overthrow it if ever they got the chance.

C. The Impact on Russia

The Russian empire was destroyed by the war and the Revolution of 1917. It lost territory to other countries.

D. Hopes for Peace

Most people hoped that there would be no more war and many countries joined the League of Nations to preserve world peace.

Europe in 1919

N = NETHERLANDS
B = BELGIUM
AL = ALSACE-LORRAINE
RL = RHINELAND
LX = LUXEMBOURG
SW = SWITZERLAND

THE LEAGUE OF NATIONS

A. *Aims*

The League of Nations was set up in 1920 (i) to preserve world peace; (ii) to prepare colonial peoples for independence and (iii) to improve living conditions throughout the world.

B. Organisation

The League was organised as follows.

1. The Assembly with representatives from all member countries met once a year to discuss problems of world concern.
2. The Council of the League made sure that the decisions of the organisation were carried out.
3. The Secretariat was the League's civil service.
4. Special agencies dealt with refugees, drug trafficking, slavery, armaments reduction, etc.

C. Achievements

1. The League settled several international disputes peacefully, e.g. between Sweden and Finland and between Poland and Lithuania.
2. It sponsored important international agreements, e.g. the Locarno treaties and the Kellogg–Briand Pact.
3. Its specialist organisations helped to improve world health, reduce slavery and supervise mandated territories (colonies being prepared for independence).
4. The League also sponsored major disarmament conferences between the great powers.

D. Defects

The League had several defects.

1. The USA never joined.
2. Germany and USSR were members for a short time only.
3. The great powers on the Council seemed to run the League and smaller states felt that they had little influence.
4. The League had no army to enforce its decisions.

E. Failure

Because of these defects, the League was unable to deal with several crises involving major powers. These included: (i) the Japanese invasion of China (1931); (ii) the Italian invasion of Ethiopia (1935); (iii) Hitler's violation of the Versailles Treaty (1933–9); (iv) the Spanish Civil War (1936–9) and (v) the Czech and Polish crises (1938, 1939).

USSR

A. The Russian Revolution

1. Russia suffered terribly during World War I.
2. In February 1917 the workers of Petrograd (the capital) went on strike and the army mutinied.

3. Tsar Nicholas II abdicated and a Provisional Government took over the country.
4. However, in November 1917 Vladimir Ilyich Lenin and a small group of Bolshevik (Communist) revolutionaries overthrew the Provisional Government.
5. A vicious civil war followed and the Communists were finally victorious in 1920.
6. After 1922, Communist controlled Russia and its territories was called the 'Union of Soviet Socialist Republics' (USSR).

V. I. Lenin

B. Communism
1. Lenin was a follower of the German philosopher Karl Marx.
2. Marx believed that exploited workers everywhere should overthrow their rulers and set up 'a classless stateless society where each would work according to his ability and receive according to his needs'.

C. Stalin
1. The USSR had been so devastated by war that Lenin was unable to create his Marxist paradise before his death in 1924.
2. This became the task of his ruthless successor, Josef Stalin, whose policies included collectivisation and the five-year plans.

D. Collectivisation
1. Collectivisation aimed to modernise Soviet agriculture and to destroy the kulaks (comparatively rich peasants), whom Stalin believed hated Communism.
2. The kulaks' small farms were confiscated and consolidated into large government-controlled collective farms. Modern techniques and machinery were introduced to increase food production.

3. The kulaks resisted but collectivisation was enforced. Millions of kulaks were killed or exiled to Siberia.

4. However, the collective farms were badly run. Food production fell drastically but Stalin refused to reverse collectivisation.

E. The Five-Year Plans

1. The Five-Year Plans aimed to make the Soviet Union a great industrial and military power.

2. Mines were opened, factories and power stations were built and millions of peasants were sent to work in the cities.

3. Although few targets laid down in the Plans were reached, the USSR did succeed in becoming one of the world's great powers.

4. However, the workers' welfare was neglected and the Five-Year Plans created a society similar to that in Western Europe during the worst days of the industrial revolution.

F. The Great Purges

1. Many Russians believed that Stalin's policies caused too much suffering and he had many rivals within the Communist Party.

2. He ordered the secret police to arrest all who had opposed him, or who might oppose him.

3. Millions were imprisoned. Some confessed to 'crimes against the state' at show trials. Many were executed without trial and about ten million died in labour camps in Siberia.

4. As a result of these purges, Stalin became the undisputed master of a terror-stricken country.

FASCIST ITALY

A. Italy 1919

Italy was on the winning side in World War I but it emerged from the fighting in a chaotic condition.

1. The army had suffered enormous losses and there were few jobs for demobilised soldiers.

2. High inflation made money worthless.

3. There was widespread disorder as peasants and workers took over lands and factories in imitation of Russia's revolutionaries. The Mafia added to the disorder in the south.

4. Governments were short-lived, inefficient and corrupt.

B. Fascists

1. Many people, especially ex-soldiers, were unhappy with these conditions.
2. In 1919 one of them, Benito Mussolini, founded an organisation of ex-servicemen, Il Fascio di Combattimento.
3. Its members were nicknamed 'Fascists' or 'Blackshirts' because of their uniform.
4. Fascists broke up strikes organised by Communists and Socialists and became popular with the middle classes, the Church and the police.
5. By 1922 the Fascists had grown powerful enough for Mussolini's supporters to demand 'a march on Rome' to take control of the country.
6. The prime minister wanted to use the army against the Fascists. Instead, the king invited Mussolini to form a government.

C. Il Duce

During the 1920s Mussolini gradually made himself dictator (Il Duce) of Italy.
1. He obtained the right to make laws without parliament.
2. He banned all political parties and trade unions other than the Fascists and his political opponents were imprisoned, killed or beaten up.
3. Books and newspapers were censored but constant propaganda was used to build up the popularity of Il Duce.

D. Achievements

Fascist Italy was often violent, corrupt and inefficient. However, Mussolini achieved several significant successes.
1. There was stable government.
2. There were no strikes and unemployment decreased.
3. New motorways, railways and housing were built.
4. The Pontine marshes were drained, wiping out malaria and providing additional fertile land.
5. The Mafia was suppressed.
6. The Lateran Treaty settled differences between Italy and the Vatican, and a Concordat (treaty) gave the Catholic Church an important position in Italian life with influence over education and marriage laws.

E. Destruction

However, Mussolini wanted Italy to be a world power.
1. He involved his country in wars in Abyssinia, Spain and Albania before joining Hitler in World War II.
2. The Italian armed forces were badly beaten.
3. The Allies invaded Italy (1943).
4. The king and the army overthrew Mussolini and he was finally killed (28 April 1945) by Communist partisans (guerrillas).

HITLER COMES TO POWER

A. Ideas

1. Adolf Hitler was born in Austria in 1889.
2. He lived in Vienna from 1904 to 1912 and picked up ideas there which remained with him throughout his life.
3. He believed that (i) Germans were a 'master-race'; (ii) Jews and Slavs were subhumans; (iii) Germans should unite in a 'Greater Germany' and (iv) they should conquer 'living space' in Eastern Europe.

B. The Weimar Republic

1. Hitler settled in Munich in 1912 and served bravely in the German army during World War I.
2. Emperor William II abdicated in November 1918 and the Reichstag (parliament) set up the Weimar Republic.
3. In 1919 the Weimar government accepted the Treaty of Versailles.
4. Like most ordinary Germans, Hitler was shocked by his country's defeat. He blamed the Weimar Republic and he determined to overthrow it, to destroy the Treaty of Versailles and to restore German greatness.

C. The Road to Power

1. Hitler joined the National Socialist German Workers' Party (Nazis) in Munich in 1919.
2. He was a powerful speaker, propagandist and organiser and he soon became the party's leader.
3. He created his own private army (SA, Stormtroopers or Brownshirts) and in 1923 he staged a putsch (revolution) in Munich in imitation of Mussolini's 'march on Rome'.
4. His putsch was easily defeated. He was imprisoned briefly and wrote his infamous book, *Mein Kampf*.
5. The Weimar Republic was fairly prosperous and stable during 1923–9 and the Nazis made very little progress.
6. However, Germany suffered greatly during the Great Depression after 1929. In successive elections more and more people voted for the Nazis, who declared that they alone could solve Germany's problems.
7. By December 1932 the Nazis were the biggest group in the Reichstag and President Hindenburg appointed Hitler chancellor.

D. Der Führer

Hitler now made himself Führer (dictator) of Germany.

1. The Reichstag passed the Enabling Act, which allowed Hitler to make any law he wished.

2. Hitler banned all political parties (except the Nazis) and trade unions.
3. The Gestapo (secret police) killed Hitler's opponents or sent them to concentration camps.
4. Hitler censored the media but made clever use of propaganda to build up popular support.

Nuremberg Rally 1935. Hitler is on the rostrum at the centre with the standards of the SA massed behind him

E. Achievements

Hitler also became popular because he (i) expanded the armed forces; (ii) reduced unemployment through public works; (iii) raised living standards and (iv) overthrew much of the Treaty of Versailles peacefully.

F. The Jews

1. Hitler believed that Jews were subhumans involved in an international plot to destroy Germany.
2. In 1935 he issued the Nuremberg Laws, which deprived Jews of their citizenship and their civil rights.
3. Jewish businesses were boycotted. Individuals were beaten or killed and the entire Jewish community experienced pogroms on occasions like the Kristallnacht.
4. Finally, millions of Jews were killed in extermination camps like Auschwitz as part of 'the final solution to the Jewish problem'.

THE ROAD TO WAR

A. Appeasement

1. Once in power, Hitler refused to pay the reparations demanded by the Treaty of Versailles.
2. He expanded the armed forces and withdrew Germany from the League of Nations.
3. During the Spanish Civil War (1936 - 1939), Hitler and Mussolini supported Franco's Nationalists while the USSR and the communist-controlled International Brigades helped the Republican government. This weakened the League of Nations, helped the Germans develop new military ideas and increased tension in Europe.

B. Towards War

1. In 1936 Hitler sent troops into the Rhineland, the demilitarised zone bordering France. The French did nothing to defend their frontier.

German expansion 1933-39

2. Encouraged by this weakness, Hitler made alliances with Italy (the Axis) and Japan (the Anti-Comintern Pact).
3. He sent help to Franco, defying the League of Nations.
4. In 1938 Austrian Nazis took over their country and invited Hitler to occupy it (Anschluss).
5. In 1938 Hitler demanded that Czechoslovakia should hand over the German-speaking Sudetenland. At Munich, Britain and France, who were supposed to be Czechoslovakia's allies, supported Hitler's demands and the Czechs had to give in.

Chamberlain, Daladier, Hitler and Mussolini at Munich

6. In March 1939 Hitler occupied the rest of Czechoslovakia. Realising that appeasement had failed, Britain and France promised to help any country threatened by Germany.
7. Hitler did not believe this promise and put pressure on Poland to hand over the Polish Corridor and Silesia.
8. The Poles resisted. Hitler feared that the Russians might support them. However, Stalin feared a German attack. On 29 August 1939 their foreign ministers signed the Nazi–Soviet non-aggression pact promising not to make war on one another and agreeing to partition Poland.
9. On 1 September the Germans invaded Poland and on 3 September Britain and France declared war on Germany.

WORLD WAR II

A. War in Europe
1. 1939: The Germans conquered Poland in a swift campaign using Blitzkrieg tactics. They then partitioned Poland with the USSR.

2. 1940: The Germans occupied Denmark, Norway, The Low Countries and France. British troops were forced to evacuate from Dunkirk. Later that year, a German attempt to bomb Britain into submission was defeated in the Battle of Britain.

3. 1941: The Germans occupied the Balkans and then invaded the USSR (Operation Barbarossa). They captured large areas of the USSR but failed to take either Leningrad or Moscow. The severe Russian winter and Russian counter-attacks caused the Germans very heavy casualties. The Germans declared war on the USA after their allies, the Japanese attacked the US base at Pearl Harbour.

4. 1942: The Germans attacked the important industrial city of Stalingrad but sustained enormous casualties before they captured it.

5. 1943: Russian forces then surrounded the Germans in Stalingrad and forced them to surrender. This was the Germans' first major defeat and they never recovered. Since 1940, Axis and British forces fought one another to control the Suez Canal. The Axis were defeated at El Alamein (1942) and surrendered at Tunis (1943). The Allies then invaded Italy. Though the Italians overthrew Mussolini and joined the Allies, German forces held out in Italy until 1945.

6. 1944: After Stalingrad, the Russians gradually forced the Germans out of the USSR and by the end of the year they were on the borders of Germany. Allied forces invaded France on D-Day (6 June) and gradually drove out the Germans. In December, a German counter-attack in the Ardennes failed (Battle of the Bulge).

7. 1945: Allied and Russian forces invaded Germany. Hitler killed himself (30 April) and the Germans surrendered unconditionally.

B. Blitzkrieg

1. The Germans used blitzkrieg (lightning war) to win the early campaigns of the war.
2. Bombers destroyed communications and bases deep behind enemy lines.
3. Next, panzer (tank) divisions smashed through fixed defences and captured important targets.
4. Finally, slow-moving infantry divisions following on cleared up the last pockets of resistance.

C. Why Germany Lost

1. As the war unfolded, Germany's enemies developed their own blitzkrieg tactics.
2. Their forces were much more numerous than the German.
3. American and Soviet war industries became more efficient and more productive than the German.

Churchill, Roosevelt and Stalin

4. Allied air forces were superior to the Luftwaffe and destroyed much of Germany's armaments industry from the air.
5. German submarines inflicted severe losses on British shipping in the early stages of the war but then US and British naval and air forces gradually overwhelmed them.

D. The War in the East

1. The Japanese invaded China in 1931.
2. After the outbreak of World War II they occupied European colonies in Indo-China, Malaya and Indonesia.
3. The Americans, who controlled the Philippines, were hostile to Japanese aggression. The Japanese feared that the Americans might attack them and struck first.
4. However, their surprise air attack on Pearl Harbour (7 December 1941) failed to destroy the US fleet.
5. The Japanese advance was halted at two great naval battles, the Coral Sea and Midway, and by the land battle of Arakhan.
6. They were then forced back towards their home islands.
7. The war ended suddenly in August 1945 when the Americans dropped atomic bombs on Nagasaki and Hiroshima, threatening the very existence of Japan.

E. The Results of the War

1. Nearly forty million people (twenty million of them Russians) were killed.
2. Many more millions were injured.
3. Many millions were forced to leave their ancestral homes and take refuge elsewhere, e.g. Germans from Eastern Europe.
4. Thousands of cities and towns were destroyed.
5. Britain, France and Japan ceased to be great powers.

6. The heavy losses inflicted on Britain and France made it impossible for them to resist their colonies' demands for independence during the 1950s and 1960s.
7. The USSR became the greatest power in Europe, controlling territory stretching into central Germany.
8. Germany no longer existed as an independent state and was divided between its enemies.
9. America became the world's greatest power, especially as it was the only country with atomic weapons.
10. Nazi leaders were tried for war crimes at Nuremberg. Some were executed or imprisoned. A few were found 'not guilty'.

14 IRELAND 1922-1990

THE IRISH FREE STATE 1922–1932

A. The Constitution
1. The Irish Free State came into existence on 6 December 1922.
2. Its Constitution described (i) the system of government and (ii) the rights of its citizens.

B. The System of Government
1. The governor general represented the monarch.
2. The Oireachtas, i.e. the Dáil and Senate, made the laws.
3. (i) The people elected the Dáil using a voting system called proportional representation (PR). (ii) PR was designed to give even small minorities representation in the Dáil.
4. The Dáil elected (i) the head of government (the president of the executive council) and (ii) some senators.

5. The president of the executive council chose (i) the ministers who made up the executive council, (ii) some senators and (iii) the governor general.
6. The senate could hold up bills for a short time only.

C. The Rights of the Citizen

1. All adult citizens could vote in Dáil elections.
2. All citizens enjoyed freedom of speech, religion and association.
3. People could not be arrested without reason and had the right to be tried in the courts.
4. All children had a right to primary education.

D. W.T. Cosgrave

1. W.T. Cosgrave and his Pro-Treaty supporters formed a party called Cumann na nGaedheal which ruled the Free State until 1932.
2. Anti-Treaty TDs did not enter the Dáil for several years and the Labour Party led the opposition to the government.

W. T. Cosgrave

E. Law and Order

1. Kevin O'Higgins had the job of restoring law and order after the Civil War.
2. He set up the unarmed Garda Síochána to replace the RIC.
3. He simplified the court system.
4. He was responsible for Public Safety Acts to deal with the IRA.

F. The Army Mutiny

1. The government reduced the army after the Civil War.
2. In March 1924 some officers demanded an end to demobilisation and more progress towards a republic.
3. O'Higgins ended the mutiny and established the custom whereby neither the army nor the gardaí interferes in the business of government.

G. Economics

1. Cosgrave and O'Higgins followed Arthur Griffith's political ideas but they rejected his economic ideas.
2. They continued the system whereby Ireland exported food to pay for industrial imports, while its surplus labour emigrated.
3. The government established semi-state companies, e.g. the Sugar Company, to stimulate agriculture and industry.
4. Cumann na nGaedheal set up the ESB and built the Shannon Scheme to provide electricity.
5. The government was more interested in balancing the budget than in developing the economy or in providing social services.
6. As a result, there was much poverty, a severe housing shortage and low health and educational standards in the Irish Free State.

H. Relations with the Commonwealth

1. Cosgrave's government worked hard to stress Ireland's independence.
2. In 1924 it persuaded the League of Nations to accept the Free State as an independent country.
3. In 1925 the Boundary Commission recommended that some territory be swapped between Northern Ireland and the Free State. This proposal was unpopular in the Free State and Cosgrave persuaded the British to ignore the recommendation.
4. At the 1926 Commonwealth Conference, the Irish delegates persuaded the British to admit that they had no authority over Commonwealth countries.
5. In 1931 the British parliament passed the Statute of Westminster. This allowed Commonwealth countries to change or repeal any laws Westminster had made for them. The Oireachtas could now change the Treaty.

FIANNA FAIL

A. The Origins of Fianna Fáil

1. De Valera and his supporters refused to enter the Dáil because of the oath of allegiance.
2. However, by 1926, it was clear that most people accepted the Free State.
3. De Valera then suggested to Sinn Féin that its TDs should enter the Dáil if the oath of allegiance were abolished.
4. The party rejected his suggestion.
5. De Valera resigned and founded Fianna Fáil (16 May 1926).

B. Aims

Fianna Fáil aimed (i) to create a thirty-two-county republic; (ii) to restore the Irish language; (iii) to develop agriculture through tillage and (iv) to develop industry with the help of protective tariffs (taxes placed on imports).

C. 'An Empty Formula'

1. Fianna Fáil won forty-four seats in a general election (June 1927).
2. The Fianna Fáil TDs refused to take the oath of allegiance and were excluded from the Dáil.
3. In August, following the murder of Kevin O'Higgins, the Oireachtas declared that from now on a person could not stand for election if he or she refused to take the oath.
4. Fianna Fáil TDs now had to take the oath or leave public life.
5. On 11 August 1927 they took the oath declaring that it was 'an empty formula' and meant nothing.

D. Victory

1. Between 1927 and 1932 Cumann na nGaedheal became very unpopular. (i) It cut the salaries of guards, teachers and civil servants. (ii) It enacted tough anti-drink laws. (iii) It appeared to be happy with the British connection. (iv) It failed to ease unemployment or emigration.
2. Fianna Fáil became popular. (i) It had radical policies to improve the economy. (ii) It intended to weaken the links with Britain. (iii) It used the *Irish Press* as an effective means of propaganda and (iv) it was very well organised throughout the country.
3. Fianna Fáil won seventy-two seats in the 1932 general election and formed a government with the help of the Labour Party.
4. Fianna Fáil governments ruled the country until 1948.

The first Fianna Fáil government which took office on 9 March 1932. Front Row: Frank Aiken (Defence),
P. J. Ruttledge (Lands and Fisheries), E. de Valera (President and External Affairs), Dr J. Ryan (Agriculture),
Tomas O Deirg (Education), J. Geoghegan (Justice). Back Row: S. MacEntee (Finance), S. T. O'Kelly
(Vice President and Local Government and Public Health), Senator J. Connolly (Post and Telegraphs), S. Lemass
(Industry and Commerce), G. Boland (Parliamentary Secretary to the President and to the Minister for Defence)

FIANNA FAIL IN GOVERNMENT 1932–1939

A. Amending the Treaty

1. Fianna Fáil in government now changed the Treaty. They (i) abolished the oath of allegiance; (ii) removed the governor general; (iii) removed all reference to the monarch from the Constitution and (iv) introduced the 1937 Constitution which made 'Ireland a republic in all but name'.
2. However, Ireland did not leave the Commonwealth, probably to avoid antagonising the British.

B. The Economic War

1. The British government had made loans to Irish farmers to buy their farms.
2. Cosgrave's government collected land annuities from the farmers to pay back the British.
3. (i) In 1932 de Valera stopped paying annuities. (ii) The British retaliated by taxing Irish goods. (iii) The Irish government retaliated in kind. (iv) Very quickly, trade between the two countries came to a standstill.
4. This economic war ruined the cattle industry. However, tillage expanded and new small industries developed to provide goods no longer imported.
5. The economies of both countries suffered badly and on 27 April 1938 Prime Minister Chamberlain and de Valera agreed (i) to settle the land annuity problem with a final payment of ten million pounds; (ii) to remove import taxes and (iii) to return the Treaty ports to Ireland.

C. Economic and Social Development

1. Seán Lemass, minister for industry and commerce, (i) set up many semi-state companies, (ii) taxed imported goods 'to protect' Irish industries and (iii) gave grants and tax breaks to new industries.
2. Many new housing estates were built.
3. Social welfare benefits were improved.

D. The Blueshirts

1. De Valera sacked Eoin O'Duffy, the garda commissioner, because of his close links with the Cosgrave government.
2. O'Duffy then (20 July 1933) became leader of the Army Comrades Association (ACA), a group of ex-soldiers.
3. He reorganised the ACA along Fascist lines with a blueshirt uniform, straight-arm salute, etc.
4. De Valera feared a coup d'état (like that Mussolini had staged in Italy) and banned the Blueshirts from marching through Dublin (12 August 1933).

Blueshirt parade

5. The Blueshirts then joined Cumann na nGaedheal and the Centre Party to form Fine Gael.
6. O'Duffy was the party's first leader but was forced to resign after encouraging farmers to hold back land annuities illegally.
7. W.T. Cosgrave then became leader of Fine Gael.
8. In 1936 O'Duffy led 600 Blueshirts to fight for Franco in the Spanish Civil War.

E. The IRA

1. At first the IRA supported de Valera believing that he would declare a republic and reunify the country.
2. He did neither and the IRA turned against him.
3. They committed several brutal murders and de Valera outlawed them (18 June 1936).

F. The Constitution of 1937

In July 1937 the people accepted a new constitution.
1. It described Éire (Ireland) as an 'independent state'.
2. It claimed jurisdiction over Northern Ireland.
3. It provided for a president to be elected by the people.
4. It set up a system of government similar to that outlined in the Constitution of 1922.
5. It guaranteed freedom of religion, speech, etc.
6. Only the people can change the Constitution in a referendum.

NORTHERN IRELAND 1920–1939

A. Divided Community

1. The Government of Ireland Act 1920 set up a parliament in Belfast to manage the internal affairs of Northern Ireland. Britain continued to control foreign affairs, taxation, the armed forces, etc.

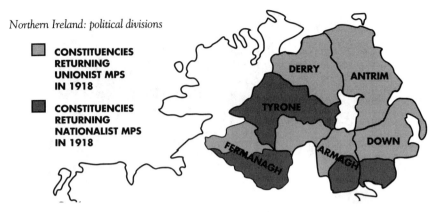

Northern Ireland: political divisions

■ **CONSTITUENCIES RETURNING UNIONIST MPS IN 1918**

■ **CONSTITUENCIES RETURNING NATIONALIST MPS IN 1918**

2. The people of Northern Ireland were a very divided community. (i) Two-thirds were unionists and Protestants loyal to Britain. (ii) One-third were nationalists and Catholics, most of whom wanted a united Ireland.

3. Many nationalists and Catholics resisted the Northern Ireland government. The government used the army and the Royal Ulster Constabulary (RUC) against them and there was considerable sectarian violence in Belfast.

B. Discrimination

1. The Northern Ireland government led by Sir James Craig (Lord Craigavon) distrusted the Catholics and nationalists and kept them out of all important public positions.

2. There was always a large unionist majority in parliament (this was unavoidable) and no nationalist or Catholic ever became a government minister.

3. Where Catholics were in a majority, e.g. Derry, the voting system for elections was gerrymandered (abused) so that unionist minorities were able to win control of local councils.

4. Nationalists and Catholics did not receive a fair share of local government housing.

5. Protestant schools received much more government support than Catholic ones.

6. The government organised an armed part-time police force called the B-Specials composed entirely of unionists. Their task was to control their Catholic and nationalist neighbours.

7. A Special Powers Act gave the government authority (i) to ban any organisation, publication or meeting and (ii) to intern any individual indefinitely, without trial.

C. Economic Depression

1. Catholics and Protestants alike experienced terrible hardship during the Great Depression of the 1930s.

2. The government did very little to help them.

3. In 1932 Belfast workers of all religions united to protest against the government's inactivity.

4. The government promised jobs – for Protestants.
5. Sectarian rioting broke out. Eleven people were killed. Six hundred were injured and the army had to restore law and order.

THE EMERGENCY

A. Neutrality
1. World War II broke out on 1 September 1939.
2. The Dáil declared that Ireland would stay neutral, i.e. that it would support neither side.
3. Most people favoured neutrality (i) to save lives; (ii) to prevent destruction and (iii) to stress the country's independence.

B. Showing Neutrality
1. There were Irish ambassadors in Axis *and* Allied countries.
2. Newspapers and radio broadcasts were censored so that they did not appear to favour either side.
3. The armed forces were greatly expanded.
4. The government interned many IRA men whose activities might cause war with Britain.

A unit of the Irish Army in 1939. Note the German-style helmets

C. Supplies
Seán Lemass was minister for supplies.
1. He organised fuel and food rationing.
2. He prosecuted those who broke the rationing regulations.
3. He set up Irish Shipping to import supplies.
4. He ordered compulsory tillage so that the country had enough wheat.

D. Not So Neutral

In practice Ireland was not neutral but helped the Allies.

1. Many Irish people worked in Britain.
2. Fifty thousand Irish people joined the British forces.
3. Allied servicemen stranded in Ireland were sent back to Britain.
4. Information about German submarines and aircraft was passed to the Allies.

NORTHERN IRELAND DURING WORLD WAR II

A. Involvement

As part of the United Kingdom, Northern Ireland was heavily involved in World War II.

1. Its factories produced ships, tanks, aeroplanes, uniforms, parachutes and tents.
2. Its farms exported food to Britain.
3. Many northerners (Catholic and Protestant) served in the British armed forces.
4. Allied troops trained in the North for D-Day.
5. Derry was an important base for anti-submarine warfare.
6. There was little unemployment and most people experienced some degree of prosperity.

B. Bombing

1. Belfast and Derry were bombed.
2. Belfast suffered many casualties and very heavy damage.
3. Fire brigades from the South helped the people of Belfast. This improved relations between North and South.
4. However, the improved relations did not last very long as unionists resented southern neutrality.

C. A New Prime Minister

1. Sir Basil Brooke (later Lord Brookeborough) became prime minister in 1943 and remained in power until 1963.
2. Brookeborough proved very efficient in organising the North's war effort.
3. However, he was a fanatical unionist and did nothing to help matters with nationalists and Catholics.

Lord Brookeborough

THE FIRST INTER-PARTY GOVERNMENT

A. 1945–1948

Fianna Fáil became very unpopular during 1945–8.

1. The government failed to help industry re-establish itself after the war.
2. There was massive unemployment and emigration.
3. Rationing continued.
4. The government seemed to be uninterested in social reform.
5. A new party, Clann na Poblachta, promised a republic and improved social conditions. This attracted many supporters away from Fianna Fáil.

B. A New Government

1. There was a general election in 1948 and Fianna Fáil lost its majority in the Dáil.
2. The other parties (Fine Gael, Labour, National Labour, Clann na Poblachta, Clann na Talmhan and some independents) united to form the first coalition or inter-party government under John A. Costello.

C. Declaring a Republic

1. Ireland became a republic and left the Commonwealth (1949) (i) 'to take the gun out of Irish politics' by giving the IRA the republic they had been fighting for and (ii) to demonstrate that Ireland was totally independent.
2. The British (i) recognised the republic; (ii) continued to treat Irish people as British citizens but (iii) guaranteed the position of Northern Ireland within the United Kingdom.

D. Other Achievements

1. The first inter-party government built many badly needed local authority houses.
2. It improved public health by wiping out TB.
3. It helped farmers to prosper by arranging favourable trading terms with Britain.

E. The Mother and Child Scheme

1. In 1951 Noël Browne, minister for health, tried to provide free treatment, hospital services and drugs for all mothers and children.

Noël Browne

2. However, (i) ministers objected to the cost; (ii) doctors objected for ethical reasons; and (iii) the Catholic bishops declared privately that the scheme was opposed to Catholic social teaching.
3. The government scrapped the scheme because of this opposition.
4. Browne resigned, blaming the bishops for what had happened.
5. The government lost its Dáil majority shortly afterwards and Fianna Fáil won the election which followed (30 May 1951).
6. Nobody took very much notice of the affair at the time. They were more concerned with unemployment and emigration.
7. Later, however, many people felt that the bishops had no right to put secret pressure on the government.

NORTHERN IRELAND: THE WELFARE STATE

A. The Welfare State
1. The Labour Party won the British general election in July 1945 and immediately set up the 'welfare state', i.e. brought in large-scale social welfare benefits.
2. The Unionist government in Belfast did not like the Labour Party or the welfare state but had to follow Britain.
3. Living conditions rapidly improved in Northern Ireland as (i) social welfare benefits increased; (ii) free secondary and university education became available; (iii) a free health service was created and (iv) many new houses were built.

B. Problems
1. Social conditions in the North were much better than in the South and Catholics and nationalists seemed to accept the system of government.
2. When southern IRA units began their border campaign in 1956, northern nationalists did not support them.
3. However, Catholics continued to suffer discrimination.
4. Unemployment was much higher among nationalists than among unionists and this caused tension between the two communities.

C. Exit Brookeborough
1. Brookeborough served the North well during World War II but he did very little after 1945 and his behaviour contributed greatly to the bad relations between Catholics and Protestants.
2. He was succeeded by Terence O'Neill (1963) who was interested in (i) economic development; (ii) healing sectarian divisions and (iii) establishing good relations between North and South.

THE LEMASS YEARS

A. 1951–1957
1. (i) Fianna Fáil won the 1951 general election. (ii) The second inter-party government came to power in 1954. (iii) Fianna Fáil formed another government in 1957.
2. Ireland experienced considerable economic hardship 1951–7 and there was much unemployment and emigration.

B. Enter Lemass
1. De Valera became president in 1959 and Seán Lemass became Taoiseach.
2. Lemass was especially interested in economics and his time as Taoiseach (1959–66) saw major developments in industry and agriculture.

C. Economic Development
1. During the 1930s Lemass tried to build up Irish industry through protectionism (taxing imports).
2. By the 1960s Lemass believed that (i) protectionism led to inefficiency and (ii) Ireland needed to gear its industries for export.
3. T.K. Whitaker drew up the 'First Programme for Economic Expansion' to develop the economy along these lines.
4. Lemass put the First Programme into action. (i) Farmers received grants to increase production. (ii) Irish industrialists were given grants to modernise their firms. (iii) Foreign companies were encouraged to set up industries. (iv) The IDA and CTT stepped up their work. (v) A trade agreement was concluded with Britain.
5. As a result of these steps: (i) many new industries were set up; (ii) unemployment fell; (iii) emigration declined and (iv) the population increased for the first time since the Famine.

D. Education
1. Education made little progress in independent Ireland.
2. Enormous talent was wasted and the country lacked a properly educated workforce to develop the economy.
3. Donogh O'Malley, minister for education (1966–8), introduced many improvements. These included: (i) free post-primary education for all; (ii) free school transport; (iii) grants for some university students and (iv) funding to build secondary schools and regional technical colleges.

E. Northern Ireland
1. Lemass was anxious to improve relations with Northern Ireland.
2. In January 1965 he visited Prime Minister Terence O'Neill in Belfast. A month later O'Neill visited Dublin.

Terence O'Neill and Seán Lemass

3.   Their efforts led to violent protests from unionists.

F.   Exit Lemass

Lemass resigned in November 1966 and Jack Lynch became Taoiseach.

NORTH AND SOUTH 1966–1993

A.   Steps Towards Reform

1.   O'Neill tried to improve relations between North and South.
2.   He also tried to improve community relations in the North by visiting Catholic schools and by meeting Catholic clergymen.
3.   However, hardline unionists thought that O'Neill was going too far and was 'betraying Ulster'.

B.   The Northern Economy

1.   The traditional northern industries declined after World War II.
2.   O'Neill tried to develop the North's economy by methods similar to those used by Lemass. He was partially successful.
3.   However, most of the North's new industries were located east of the Bann and profited unionists mainly.
4.   O'Neill helped to found the new town of Craigavon and the New University of Ulster at Coleraine. Because of their location, these were seen as benefiting unionists only.

C.   The Civil Rights Movement

1.   During the 1960s Martin Luther King led the coloured people of the USA to victory in a peaceful campaign to secure civil rights.
2.   In February 1967 Catholics and nationalists in Northern Ireland founded the Northern Ireland Civil Rights Association (NICRA) to secure equality in politics, employment and housing.
3.   In October 1968 the RUC used great violence to break up a NICRA demonstration in Derry.

4. The event was shown on television throughout the world. The British government was very embarrassed and forced O'Neill to promise reforms.
5. O'Neill's promises were too little to satisfy Catholics and too much for unionists.
6. Sectarian strife increased and O'Neill resigned in April 1969 when he was unable to win the support of Unionist MPs.

D. The Summer of '69

1. In August 1969 a unionist procession through Derry led to fierce rioting in which the RUC and B-Specials showed themselves to be strongly pro-unionist.
2. Later, unionist mobs attacked Catholic areas of Belfast. Once again the police supported the unionists.
3. Six Catholics were killed and 150 houses were destroyed.
4. The North was on the brink of civil war and James Callaghan, the British home secretary, ordered the British army to restore peace and to protect Catholics.

E. Reaction in the South

1. From 1966 to 1969 Jack Lynch was more concerned with economic problems in the Republic than he was with the North.
2. The events of August 1969 caused him to declare that the Irish government could 'no longer stand by' while nationalist communities were being attacked.
3. Beyond taking in refugees, the Irish government did nothing.
4. Some ministers wanted more vigorous action.
5. Lynch dismissed two of them, Charles J. Haughey and Neil Blaney (a third, Kevin Boland, resigned in sympathy).
6. Haughey and Blaney were later tried for gun-running. They were found 'not guilty'.

F. Internment

1. The IRA played little part in events until 1970. Some members wanted to set up a socialist republic, others thought they now had a chance to drive the British out of Ireland. The IRA and Sinn Féin eventually split on the matter into Official and Provisional wings.
2. Meanwhile, extreme unionists formed the Ulster Defence Association (UDA) which began to kill nationalists.
3. The Provisional IRA in its turn began to shoot soldiers, policemen and unionists.
4. The army reacted violently against nationalists and many turned to the IRA for protection.
5. Brian Faulkner, prime minister of Northern Ireland, persuaded the British government to bring in internment.
6. On 9 August 1971 the security forces rounded up 300 suspects. They included no unionist terrorists and the IRA won even more support in nationalist areas.

*Bloody Sunday, Derry 1972. The clergyman at the centre of the
photograph subsequently became Bishop of Derry*

G. Bloody Sunday

1. On 30 January 1972 British paratroopers killed thirteen marchers during a civil rights demonstration in Derry.
2. A wave of anger swept through the Republic and demonstrators burned down the British embassy.
3. Northern Ireland was out of control. On 30 March 1972 Edward Heath, the British prime minister, closed down the Northern Ireland parliament and appointed William Whitelaw to rule the North directly.

H. The EEC

1. Ireland first applied to join the EEC in 1961 but was rejected.
2. However, the country eventually joined in January 1973.
3. Agriculture expanded rapidly.
4. Some industries prospered as they exploited new markets in Europe.
5. Others declined because they were not competitive enough.
6. Over the years, huge amounts of EEC aid poured into the country to develop roads, education, etc.
7. Jack Lynch called a general election in February 1973.
8. Fianna Fáil lost. A Fine Gael–Labour coalition took over with Liam Cosgrave as Taoiseach and Brendan Corish as Tánaiste.

I. Sunningdale

1. The British hoped that direct rule in Northern Ireland would not last long.
2. In June 1973 a new Assembly was elected in the North.
3. In December the British persuaded the Unionists, the Social Democratic and Labour Party and the Alliance Party to form a Power-Sharing Executive.
4. In order to satisfy nationalists, power-sharing was given an Irish dimension when a Council of Ireland was established under the Sunningdale Agreement.

5. In May 1974 unionist workers staged a general strike in opposition to power-sharing and the Sunningdale Agreement.

6. Harold Wilson's Labour government seemed afraid of the strikers and the Power-Sharing Executive and the Sunningdale Agreement collapsed. The British had to resume direct rule.

J. Political Crisis

The violence of the North spilled over into the Republic.

1. In 1974 unionist terrorists planted bombs in Dublin and Monaghan killing 31 people and injuring 150 (17 May).

2. In 1976 the IRA murdered the British ambassador in Dublin.

3. Cosgrave's coalition government brought in strict laws against the IRA and unionist terrorists.

4. President Cearbhall Ó Dálaigh thought that these laws might be unconstitutional and referred them to the Supreme Court.

5. Paddy Donegan, the minister for defence, declared that the president was a 'thundering disgrace' (18 October 1976).

6. The president resigned 'to protect the dignity of the presidency' and the coalition government became very unpopular.

K. A Succession of Governments

1. Fianna Fáil defeated the Coalition in the 1977 election.

2. The following governments have been in power in the Republic since then: (i) Fianna Fáil under Jack Lynch (1977–9) and C.J. Haughey (1979–81); (ii) Fine Gael–Labour coalition (1981–2); (iii) Fianna Fáil under C.J. Haughey (1982); (iv) Fine Gael–Labour coalition under Garret FitzGerald (1982–7); (v) Fianna Fáil under C.J. Haughey (1987–9); (vi) Fianna Fáil–Progressive Democrat coalition under C.J. Haughey (1989–92) and Albert Reynolds (1992); (vii) Fianna Fáil–Labour coalition under Albert Reynolds (1993–).

3. During this time the Republic has faced serious economic problems. These included: (i) increasing unemployment and emigration; (ii) high taxes and (iii) very high oil prices.

4. None of the steps taken by various governments seems to have had much impact on the problems.

L. Hunger-Strike

1. Margaret Thatcher's Conservative government came to power in Britain in 1979.

2. Mrs Thatcher was determined to crush the IRA.

3. She refused to allow IRA prisoners to wear their own clothes in jail.

4. The prisoners reacted by staging dirty protests in their cells and by going on hunger-

strike. Bobby Sands, the most famous hunger-striker, died on 5 May 1981 after a sixty-six-day fast.

5. Mrs Thatcher refused to back down and the hunger-strike was called off in October 1981 after ten men had died.

M. *The Hillsborough Agreement*

1. In November 1985 the British and Irish governments concluded the Hillsborough Agreement.
2. The British agreed to improve conditions for nationalists in return for greater security cooperation from the South.
3. An Inter-Governmental Conference of ministers was established to discuss northern problems on a regular basis. A permanent secretariat of Irish and British civil servants was created to support the Conference.
4. The unionists were furious at the involvement of the southern government in northern affairs. Their politicians reject the Agreement and their terrorist groups continue to murder Catholics and nationalists.
5. The IRA has also ignored the Agreement and continues to bomb and kill.

15 SOCIAL CHANGES IN TWENTIETH-CENTURY IRELAND

LIFE IN RURAL IRELAND

A. Numbers

1. At the beginning of the twentieth century most Irish people lived in the countryside.
2. Since then the rural population has declined and there are many areas which have become almost totally depopulated.
3. However, the urban population has grown and most Irish people now live in towns.

B. Housing

1. There were many poor farm labourers in Ireland in the 1900s. They lived in small, mud-walled, dirt-floored, thatched cottages, usually with two rooms. Nearly all these cottages have since been abandoned. At this time the government built many stone cottages on acre-plots for farm labourers. Many of these cottages are still used but have been greatly modernised.

2. 'Small' farmers occupied large cottages with more rooms and stone floors.
3. Most 'strong' farmers owned two-storey slated houses. These houses sometimes had 'parlours', which were wallpapered and fitted out with shop-bought furniture. They were used only on special occasions.
4. Many ex-landlords continued to occupy 'big houses' with numerous rooms. Those occupied by the family were large, well-proportioned and lavishly decorated. The staff had to be satisfied with small pokey quarters.
5. As farmers became richer, they refurbished their houses or replaced them with modern bungalows.
6. Very few country houses had indoor water, toilets or bathrooms in the 1900s. Even in 1946 less than half of the rural population enjoyed these facilities.
7. Most furniture was made locally. Cottages had a few stools or chairs with súgán backs and seats and some wooden-framed beds. Many poor people had no tables or dressers. They ate from plates held on their laps and their few cooking appliances were stored in niches in the walls.
8. Rural electrification came in the 1950s. Houses suddenly became brighter and electrical equipment such as cookers and cleaners made them cleaner and healthier. Electric pumps provided an indoor water supply.

C. Work
1. In the 1900s most farm work was carried out by hand or with the help of horses. Few horses are now used on farms and machinery performs many tasks that were once done by hand. These tasks include milking, ploughing, harvesting, threshing, reaping and binding.
2. In the 1900s women often helped the men on the land, especially in the poorer areas where horses and ploughs were not available. They looked after poultry, gathered seaweed for fertiliser, cooked food, baked bread, cured bacon, made butter, carried water, cleaned the house, reared the children, mended clothes, took care of sick animals and people, worked on the bog . . . Although machinery has greatly eased many of these tasks, women still carry out a huge amount of work in rural Ireland.

D. Entertainment
1. For many years, entertainment was home-made.
2. People visited one another's houses to exchange news, to tell stories, to play cards, to attend 'stations' (house masses) or to play music and dance.
3. Gaelic football, hurling, bowling and coursing were also favourite pastimes, while the 'quality' played golf or croquet, went fox-hunting or attended house dances.
4. Radio became very popular during the 1930s, especially broadcasts of sporting events like the All-Ireland hurling and football finals.
5. During this period fit-ups (travelling theatres and cinemas) played in village halls or barns for a few nights before moving on to their next venue.

6. Crossroads dancing and barn dances were common and dance-halls became fashionable during the 1920s.

7. Many amateur drama groups were set up during the 1950s and local drama festivals were a very popular entertainment.

8. Organisations such as Macra na Tuaithe (now Foróige), Macra na Feirme and the ICA helped people to develop hobbies, to take part in public speaking, quizzes, debates, etc.

LIFE IN THE TOWNS

A. Housing

1. In the 1900s many of Ireland's urban poor lived in small cottages strung out along the approach roads or in the back lanes of the towns.

2. Their cottages were similar to those of the farm labourers and few had running water or toilets.

Dublin slums c. 1900

3. (i) The poor of the big cities lived in tenements, i.e. decayed houses which had once belonged to the rich. (ii) Usually, a family occupied a single room and sometimes sublet a corner to a lodger. (iii) Tenements were filthy, noisy and unsafe. There was little sanitation, often just one toilet and one tap per tenement. Disease was rampant.

4. (i) In the 1900s local authorities and private companies built terraces of artisans' dwellings to replace the tenements. (ii) Their rents tended to be high and only relatively well-paid craftsmen could afford them.

5. In modern times the tenements have been replaced, by blocks of flats, individual houses and suburban housing estates.

6. (i) In country towns, shopkeepers and professional people lived in large houses near the town centre or in apartments over their shops and offices. (ii) These houses and apartments were usually well furnished and many had running water, indoor toilets and bathrooms. Some even had electricity.

New housing at Ballymun, Dublin

7. In the cities, middle-class business and professional people lived in the suburbs, away from the noise and dirt of the city centre. They lived in detached or semi-detached houses, often with gardens. Most middle-class families had servants.

Middle class housing, Dublin

B. Work

1. Until recently, craftsmen living in Irish towns were usually certain of employment.
2. There were always many unskilled labourers. During the 1900s they were employed on a daily basis and often experienced long periods of unemployment.
3. Trade union activity and better social welfare greatly improved the quality of their lives but nowadays machinery has significantly reduced their chances of obtaining employment.
4. Townswomen worked mainly at home though many from the poorer classes worked as domestic servants or in factories. Very few entered the professions and fewer still reached any prominent position until the latter half of the century.

Cork c. 1900.
Note the absence of crowds and traffic

A traffic jam in Dublin. Contrast this scene with that
on the left

C. Entertainment

1. For most of the twentieth century, townspeople, like country people, had to make their own entertainment.

. 2. The large towns had theatres which put on shows ranging from popular music-hall turns to grand opera.

3. Ireland's first cinema, the Volta, opened in 1909 and most towns eventually had one or two.

4. Dance-halls became popular in the 1920s.

5. However, cinemas (though not theatres) declined when television became available in the 1960s, and discos replaced dance-halls.

6. Sport tended to be less popular in the towns than in the country, and where it was played it tended to be soccer or rugby rather than football or hurling.

TRANSPORT AND COMMUNICATIONS

A. Land Transport

1. In the 1900s, most people walked short journeys.

2. Longer journeys were made by bicycle, by pony and trap or by side-car.

3. Railways were widely used and few places were more than 20 km from a railway station.

4. There were very few motor cars in Ireland in the 1900s because they were very expensive. However, various transport companies began to provide lorries and buses for public use.

5. In towns, people walked, cycled or travelled by tram. Buses gradually replaced trams.

6. Cars and lorries became more plentiful, especially in the 1960s. As a result, many railway lines closed down so that now only a few large towns are linked by rail.

B. Air Transport

1. Harry Ferguson carried out Ireland's first aeroplane flight in 1909.

2. In 1928 Colonel James Fitzmaurice of the Air Corps carried out the first East-West crossing of the Atlantic.

3. Aer Lingus was established in 1936.

4. Dublin Airport was opened in 1940.

5. During the 1940s flying-boats regularly flew across the Atlantic from Foynes on the Shannon.

6. Large, land-based aircraft replaced the flying boats after World War II and an airport was built at Shannon to service them.

7. Later, as the use of Shannon Airport slackened off, a duty-free area, new town and industrial estate grew up.

C. Radio and Television

1. Ireland's first radio station, 2RN opened in 1926.

2. RTE television made its first broadcast in 1961.

3. Over the years radio and television have entertained and informed the people of Ireland and made them aware of the wider world.

WOMEN IN IRISH SOCIETY

A. The 1900s

1. Women carried out a wide variety of tasks in Ireland in the 1900s but had few rights. They could not vote and their husbands took over their property when they married.

2. Although the universities and the professions were open to women, social pressures made it almost impossible for them to follow any career outside the home.

B. After Independence

1. Women played an important part in the War of Independence.
2. The Constitution of 1922 gave the vote to all citizens and declared that all were equal before the law.
3. However, laws passed during the 1920s and 1930s excluded them from juries, forced married women to give up their jobs in the public service and gave them less pay for doing the same work as men.
4. There was no women's movement to protest against this discrimination and some of the laws were removed only when men were unavailable to do necessary work (e.g. teaching).
5. Since the 1960s, the women's movement has highlighted many ways in which women suffer discrimination and cases brought under the Constitution have led to the emancipation of women in many areas of life.
6. Following the 1992 general election there are still only twenty women TDs (even though there are more women voters than men).
7. However, more women have been appointed to important political jobs than ever before and the election of Mary Robinson as president of the Republic must be a sign of things to come.

NOTE: YOU MUST STUDY EITHER 16A OR 16B.

16A THE SUPERPOWERS

THE BEGINNINGS OF HOSTILITY

The USA and the USSR emerged from World War II as the most powerful countries in the world. Their huge populations, infinite resources and nuclear weapons gave them a status above that of any other power, the status of 'Superpowers'.

A. The End of World War II

1. Although the USA and the USSR were allied against Germany in World War II, they distrusted one another deeply.
2. The Soviets feared that the Americans intended to stamp out Communism while the Americans believed that the Soviets wanted to impose Communism on the entire world.
3. To avoid the possibility of conflict, they agreed that Soviet troops should occupy Germany east of the Elbe and that US, British and French troops should occupy the rest of Germany.
4. The Allies also decided to divide Berlin into four 'sectors' of occupation, one for each of the four powers.

Europe after 1945

B. USSR and Germany

1. The USSR had suffered enormous casualties during World War II and it took revenge on eastern Germany.
2. Many thousands of people were rounded up and sent to forced labour camps in the Soviet Union.
3. The countryside was stripped of food and almost all the area's industries were destroyed.

C. The Iron Curtain

1. In order to protect the USSR further, Stalin stationed Soviet troops in all Eastern European countries and forced the people to elect Communist governments.
2. At the same time, he built an 'iron curtain' of barbed-wire fences, minefields and machine-gun posts stretching in an unbroken line from the Baltic to the Adriatic.

D. The Truman Doctrine

1. In 1946 civil war broke out in Greece between Communists and supporters of the king.
2. At first the British supported the royalists but by 1947 they were unable to provide any more aid.
3. Harry S. Truman, the US president, now sent help to Greece.
4. He also announced the 'Truman Doctrine', which declared that the USA would help anyone who was fighting against Communism.

E. Marshall Aid

1. In 1947 General George Marshall, the US secretary of state, announced that the USA would support all countries willing to cooperate to develop their economies.
2. The Americans hoped that the Marshall Plan would create a prosperous Europe, hostile to Communism.
3. Stalin saw the Plan as an attempt to isolate the USSR and he forbade the Communist countries of Eastern Europe to participate.

F. The Cold War

1. The period from the Berlin Blockade (1949) until the collapse of Communism (1990) is known as the 'Cold War'.
2. During this time the USA and the USSR built up (i) huge military forces and (ii) vast quantities of atomic weapons.
3. They competed in a 'space race'.
4. They also backed opposing factions in Africa, the Middle East and South-East Asia.
5. Sometimes they became actively involved in conflicts, e.g. the USA in Korea (1950–3) and Vietnam (1961–75) and the USSR in Afghanistan (1979–88).

THE BERLIN BLOCKADE

A. The Revival of Germany

1. Between 1945 and 1947 the World War II Allies deliberately kept Germany weak.
2. However, in 1947 the Western Allies realised that a backward Germany would strain their resources and would hold back the development of Europe.
3. They decided to extend the Marshall Plan to their zones and sectors of occupation to help the Germans revive their economy.

B. The Berlin Blockade

1. Stalin saw this as a threat to the USSR. He cut the overland supply links with West Berlin, hoping that this would drive the Western Allies out of the city.

2. The Western Allies feared that Stalin was trying to force Berlin into the Soviet zone and they determined to defeat him by supplying the city from the air.
3. Beginning in July 1948, the Allied air forces kept Berlin supplied with the necessities of life.
4. In May 1949 it was clear that the Allies and the Berliners would never give in and, rather than risk a war, Stalin lifted the blockade.

C. Results of the Blockade
The Berlin Blockade had several results.
1. The USA and its friends formed a military alliance (North Atlantic Treaty Organisation, NATO) to resist Soviet aggression (1949).
2. The Western Powers allowed their zones to unite as the Federal Republic of Germany and the Soviets formed their zone into the German Democratic Republic.
3. Federal Germany created an army in 1955 and joined NATO.
4. This encouraged the Soviets to form a military alliance with the Communist countries of Eastern Europe, the Warsaw Pact.
5. West Germany was more prosperous than East and many people from East Germany escaped through West Berlin.
6. In 1961 the East Germans built the Berlin Wall around West Berlin to stop such escapes. It remained until November 1989.

The Berlin Wall

The Korean War
Background
1. During World War II American forces liberated South Korea from the Japanese while Russian forces liberated North Korea.
2. The Americans set up a democratic government in the south led by Syngman Rhee.

UN Intervention
1. In June 1950, Northern forces invaded South Korea.
2. It is still uncertain whether Stalin encouraged this invasion to make up for his failure in Berlin or if it was due to Mao Tse Tung.
3. President Truman asked the United Nations to send troops to defend South Korea. The Russians were then boycotting the UN and so failed to veto the despatch of UN troops to Korea.
4. Troops from many countries fought against the Communists. However, most were American and the supreme commander was General Douglas MacArthur.

The Fighting
1. By September the North Koreans had conquered most of Korea.
2. Then UN troops landed deep behind North Korean lines. The invaders were quickly driven out of South Korea.
3. MacArthur then invaded North Korea. The Chinese feared that UN forces would push on into China and in October they entered the war on the side of the North Koreans.
4. The UN forces were now driven south and months of fighting followed around the 38th parallel.
6. MacArthur wanted to use atomic weapons in an invasion of China but Truman did not want to widen the war and sacked MacArthur.
7. Peace talks lasted from July 1951 to July 1953 when the two countries returned to their pre-war positions pending a final peace treaty, which has yet to be signed.

THE CUBAN CRISIS

A. Khrushchev
1. Stalin died in 1953 and Nikita Khrushchev became leader of the USSR.
2. He relaxed the harsh Soviet system of government, released political prisoners, tried to improve living conditions and publicly denounced Stalin's actions.

3. This encouraged East Germans, Poles and Hungarians to rebel against their Communist governments. Each rising was put down by Soviet troops.

4. Although Khrushchev worked hard to avoid direct conflict with the U.S.A., such a conflict erupted in 1962 during the Cuban missile crisis.

B. Cuba

1. Cuba lies 160 km south of Florida.

2. For years it had been a 'banana republic', a puppet of the USA, which owned an enormous naval base at Guantanamo.

3. During the 1950s Cuba was controlled by a corrupt, brutal dictator, General Fulgencio Batista.

4. In 1956 Fidel Castro began a guerrilla war which forced Batista to flee Cuba in 1959.

5. Castro introduced numerous social and economic reforms and confiscated American firms without compensation.

6. The US government retaliated by refusing to buy Cuban sugar (the country's main export) and Castro turned to Nikita Khrushchev and the USSR for assistance.

7. In 1961 the USA landed 1,500 anti-Castro Cubans at the Bay of Pigs, hoping that this invasion would spark off an anti-Castro revolt.

8. It didn't and the invasion was easily defeated.

Nikita Khrushchev

Fidel Castro

C. The Verge of War

1. The Soviets poured military advisers and equipment into Cuba.

2. American spy-planes revealed that this equipment included guided missiles which brought nearly all the major cities of the USA within range of Soviet nuclear weapons.

3. (i) On 22 October 1962 President John F. Kennedy announced that the US could not tolerate this situation. (ii) He declared that the USA would blockade Cuba to prevent the importation of more weapons. (iii) He threatened that the USA would attack the USSR if any missiles were launched against the USA.

4. Soviet ships bound for Cuba turned for home on 24 October and on 26 October Khrushchev agreed to remove the missiles from Cuba if the USA promised not to invade the island.

D. Results of the Cuban Crisis
1. Both sides were badly shocked by the crisis that had brought them so close to war.
2. To prevent future crises a 'hot line' communications network was set up between Washington and Moscow.
3. The Soviets and the Americans opened talks to reduce nuclear and conventional arms.
4. The USA continues to boycott Cuba.

THE BREZHNEV YEARS

A. The Fall of Khrushchev
1. Khrushchev's failure to deal with the Americans or to revive the Soviet economy led to his downfall in 1964.
2. He was succeeded as leader by Leonid Brezhnev.

B. The Brezhnev Years
1. Brezhnev was not as tolerant as Khrushchev. Dissidents (those who disagreed with the government) were sent to prison camps or mental hospitals.
2. In 1968 Alexander Dubcek of Czechoslovakia tried to introduce 'Communism with a human face' into his country.
3. Brezhnev ordered the Soviet army into Czechoslovakia and removed Dubcek.
4. In the 'Brezhnev Doctrine' the Soviet leader claimed the right to intervene in any country where a Communist government seemed in danger.

Russian forces crush the 'Prague Spring'

C. Towards Peace

1. In spite of Brezhnev's reputation as a hardliner, he took important steps to halt the spread of nuclear weapons.
2. 1963: Under the Test Ban Treaty the USA and USSR agreed not to test nuclear weapons in the air, in space or underwater.
3. 1968: Nuclear powers agreed in the Non-Proliferation Treaty not to help non-nuclear powers to develop nuclear weapons.
4. 1972/1990: The SALT (Strategic Arms Limitation Talks) 1 and 2 Agreements restricted the number of missiles owned by the USA and USSR.

THE END OF THE COLD WAR

A. Mikhail Gorbachev

1. Brezhnev died in 1982 and Mikhail Gorbachev became leader of the USSR in 1985.
2. Gorbachev wished to end the Cold War and to improve living conditions in the USSR.
3. He followed a policy of 'glasnost' (openness) and 'perestroika' (reform).
4. He closed down prison camps, released dissidents, granted freedom of religion, ended censorship, tried to develop an open economy, withdrew Soviet troops from Afghanistan and declared that he would not use Soviet troops to protect unpopular Communist regimes.

B. The End of the Cold War

1. During 1989 the people of Eastern Europe took advantage of this situation to overthrow their Communist masters and set up democratic governments.
2. On the night of 9 November 1989 the people of Berlin tore down the wall that divided their city.
3. The people of East Germany now demanded union with West Germany.
4. The Poles and Soviets feared a revived Germany but accepted unification when the Germans promised to accept the frontiers fixed in 1945.
5. On 2 October 1990 the two Germanies united and on 2 November they held their first free election since 1933. The Cold War was over.

THE UNITED NATIONS

A. Aims

1. The United Nations Organisation (UNO) was founded in 1944 to continue the work of the League of Nations.
2. UNO aims (i) to preserve world peace; (ii) to prepare colonies for independence and (iii) to promote the welfare of the human race.

B. Organisation

UNO is organised as follows.

1. Representatives from each member state meet in the General Assembly to discuss world problems.
2. The Security Council is supposed to preserve the peace of the world. Each of its five permanent members (USA, USSR, Britain, France, China) has a veto over the Council's decisions.
3. The Secretariat is UNO's civil service.
4. Special agencies, e.g. UNESCO, UNICEF, WHO, deal with specific social problems on a world scale.

C. Achievements

1. At one time it seemed that UNO would become another battleground between the USA and USSR and their allies. They often vetoed one another's proposals in the Security Council and so made any action by UNO almost impossible.
2. The General Assembly and Secretaries General have intervened to deal with world crises when the Security Council was deadlocked, e.g. Korea (1950–3), Suez (1956), the Congo (1960–1), Cyprus (1964).
3. UNO's specialised agencies have often helped to cope with disasters, e.g. the refugee problem in the Middle East and the famine in Somalia.

16B EUROPEAN UNITY

EARLY ATTEMPTS

A. The Impact of World War II

After World War II Europe was no longer at the centre of world power and influence. Many European leaders realised that Europe would no longer be important in world affairs unless it forgot its ancient quarrels and united.

B. Early Groupings

1. The Organisation for European Economic Cooperation (OEEC) was set up to distribute Marshall Aid and to plan the long-term economic development of Europe.
2. The Western European Union (WEU) was set up to oppose Communism (1948). The WEU joined NATO (1949) and West Germany became a member in 1955.

3. The Council of Europe was set up to develop social, cultural and economic links between the countries of Western Europe. However, it failed to become a parliament for Western Europe, as Henri Spaak, its first president, hoped.

THE EUROPEAN COMMUNITY

A. European Coal and Steel Community
1. In 1951 Belgium, France, Germany, Italy, The Netherlands and Luxembourg set up the European Coal and Steel Community (ECSC).
2. The Community set up a High Authority to plan coal and steel production. These commodities were allowed to move tax-free throughout the Community.
3. The ECSC hoped to make war impossible by interlinking the economies of the various states.

B. The Treaty of Rome
1. In 1957 the members of the ECSC signed the Treaty of Rome and formed the European Economic Community (EEC).

Signing the Treaty of Rome

2. The EEC aimed to remove all tariff barriers between its members so that goods, services and labour could pass freely between them.
3. The EEC hoped that this would improve living standards as goods became cheaper and increase employment as the various countries developed wider markets for their goods.
4. Europe's strengthened economy would then be able to compete with larger economic units like the USA and USSR. Eventually the EEC might evolve into a fully united Europe.
5. All members must contribute to a common budget and this money is used to pay for the institutions of the EEC, to support payments to farmers and to develop the more backward areas of the Community.

C. The EEC Expands

1. Britain, with its American and Commonwealth links, did not wish to join an organisation as tightly integrated as the EEC.
2. In 1959 Britain, the Scandinavian countries, Switzerland, Austria and Portugal formed the European Free Trade Association (EFTA).
3. EFTA's success was limited and in 1961 Britain applied to join the EEC.
4. However, the British wanted to impose so many conditions on their entry that Charles de Gaulle, the president of France, vetoed their application.
5. Ireland, which applied to join the EEC at the same time, was rejected as well.
6. De Gaulle resigned in 1969 and Britain, Ireland and Denmark applied for admission to the EEC again. This time their applications were successful and they became members on 1 January 1973.
7. Greece became a member in 1981 and in 1986 Spain and Portugal joined the Community.

D. EEC to EU

1. The Single European Act changed the Treaty of Rome by removing the last restrictions on free trade and by introducing a form of majority voting on the Council of Ministers. These changes were marked by a change in name, from European Economic Community (EEC) to European Community (EC) to European Union (EU).
2. In February 1992 the leaders of the EU signed the Maastricht Treaty. The Treaty declared that (i) the EU should have a common currency; (ii) the EU should adopt common foreign and security policies; (iii) the powers of the European Parliament should be enlarged.
3. Strains have developed within the EU. (i) In 1992 France and Germany failed to help fellow members during an economic crisis. (ii) Many British MPs and people resent giving more power to the EU. (iii) Poorer members, e.g. Ireland, fear a loss of benefits if poor countries from Eastern Europe join the EU.

E. The Institutions of the EU

The following institutions were set up to help fulfil the aims of the Treaty of Rome.

1. The European Parliament (i) debates the problems of interest to the Community. (ii) However, it cannot make laws. (iii) At first it consisted of MPs from the various parliaments but (iv) direct elections have been held since 1979.
2. (i) The Council of Ministers consists of ministers from each country relating to a particular activity (e.g. agriculture). (ii) The Council makes decisions but it is up to the Commission to carry them out. (iii) However, the Commission makes suggestions to the Council about the policies it wants to see enforced.

3. (i) The Court of Justice decides whether rules made by the EU are in keeping with the Treaty of Rome. (ii) It deals with disputes between members of the Community. (iii) It can declare laws made by the member states invalid if they conflict with the Treaty of Rome.
4. The Commission consists of officials appointed by the member states of the Community. Their task is to carry out the decisions of the Council but they have a very strong influence over these decisions.

AN ROINN OIDEACHAIS AGUS EOLAÍOCHTA

JUNIOR CERTIFICATE EXAMINATION 2001

HISTORY — HIGHER LEVEL

(180 Marks)

FRIDAY, 8 JUNE — AFTERNOON, 2.00 to 4.30

Answer *all* questions, **1**, **2** and **3** in the appropriate spaces on the examination paper.

1. **PICTURES** (15 marks)

Study the pictures A1, A2, B, C1 and C2 which accompany this paper and then answer the following questions.

(a) **PICTURES A1 AND A2**

Picture A1 shows a High Cross. Picture A2 shows a Round Tower.

A1

A2

(i)   What was the usual subject matter of the carvings on High Crosses such as in Picture A1?   (1)

(ii)   In Picture A2, why do you think the entrance (marked X) was built so high off the ground?   (2)

(iii) Name an early Christian site in Ireland where you would find an example of each of the following:
(a) A High Cross:
(b) A Round Tower: (2)

(b) **PICTURE B**

Picture B is a detail from a painting called The School of Athens *by Raphael.*

B

(i)   This picture was painted during the Renaissance. Give **two** pieces of evidence from the picture to support this statement.   (2)

(ii)   Name **one** Renaissance painter who was not from Italy and name **one** of his works.
Painter:
Work: (2)

(c) **PICTURES C1 AND C2**

Pictures C1 and C2 are election posters from the 1932 general election in Ireland.

(i) How does Picture C1 argue that you should **not** vote for Fianna Fáil? (1)

(ii) Name **one** of the problems that Picture C2 suggests Ireland faced at that time. (1)

(iii) In addition to Fianna Fáil and Cumann na nGaedheal, name **one** party that contested the general election in 1932. (2)

(iv) Name the leaders of Fianna Fáil and Cumann na nGaedheal in 1932.

Fianna Fáil:

Cumann na nGaedheal: (2)

2. DOCUMENTS (15 marks)

Read the two documents, **1** and **2**, which accompany this paper and then answer the following questions.

(a) **DOCUMENT 1**

This is an extract from the *Proclamation of the Irish Republic* issued by the leaders of the 1916 Rising.

IRISHMEN AND IRISHWOMEN: In the name of God and of the dead generations from which she receives her old tradition of nationhood, Ireland, through us, summons her children to her flag and strikes for her freedom.

Having organised and trained her manhood through her secret revolutionary organisation, the Irish Republican Brotherhood, and through her open military organisations, the Irish Volunteers and the Irish Citizen Army, having patiently perfected her discipline . . . supported by her exiled children in America and by gallant allies in Europe, but relying in the first on her own strength, she strikes in full confidence of victory.

The Irish Republic is entitled to, and hereby claims, the allegiance of every Irishman and Irishwoman. The Republic guarantees religious and civil liberty, equal rights and equal opportunities to all its citizens, and declares its resolve to pursue the happiness and prosperity of the whole nation and all its parts, cherishing all of the children of the nation equally, and oblivious of the differences carefully fostered by an alien government, which have divided a minority from the majority in the past.

We place the cause of the Irish Republic under the protection of the Most High God, Whose blessing we invoke upon our arms, and we pray that no one who serves that cause will dishonour it by cowardice, inhumanity or rapine.

(i)   From whom does Ireland receive her 'old tradition of nationhood'?   (1)

(ii)   Name **one** of the groups that 'organised and trained her manhood'.   (1)

(iii) Give **one** piece of evidence to show that the Rising received support from outside of Ireland.   (1)

(iv)   What does the document accuse the 'alien government' of doing?   (1)

(v)   Give **two** pieces of evidence from this extract to show how the leaders hoped that this document would encourage people to support the Rising. (2)

(vi)   Name **two** of the leaders executed for their part in the 1916 Rising.   (2)

(b) DOCUMENT 2

These are extracts from two newspapers from Northern Ireland about the introduction of Direct Rule into Northern Ireland in 1972. A is from the *Irish News* and B is from the *Newsletter*.

A. Irish News, Saturday, March 25th, 1972.

The experiment of a suspended Stormont, and administration by a Westminster Secretary of State who will have the assistance of a local commission, will be watched with interest far beyond our shores . . .

In this new arrangement, the minority will remain the minority, but their political ideas can be expressed more freely without the shadow of the Special Powers Act falling across them. They can feel some satisfaction that the weakness of permanent Unionist rule has at last been recognised.

But they will be asking if Mr Heath [the British Prime Minister] in dismantling Stormont which was designed to ensure Protestant ascendancy [control], has also recognised that the day must come when Ireland will be united under an all-Ireland government.

B. Newsletter, March 25th, 1972.

Betrayal is a bitter, dangerous word that is not used carelessly except in anger . . . . No assurances that Mr Edward Heath may give or has given, as to the duration of the suspension of Stormont, or on any other matter dealing with the future of the province, will remove that word from the minds of at least one million British citizens here.

For close on 50 years the Northern Ireland Government . . . succeeded in maintaining stability and in the main the full safety of its people. It was only when our defences were deliberately smashed by Westminster that the floodgate was opened for the terrorist and the criminal.

Source: *The Past from the Press*, The National Library of Ireland.

(i)   With what was the 'suspended Stormont' to be replaced?   (1)
(ii)   What had prevented the minority from expressing their ideas freely?   (1)
(iii)   What does the *Irish News* feel that Stormont was designed to ensure?   (1)
(iv)   What is the attitude of the *Newsletter* to the introduction of Direct Rule? Give **one** piece of evidence from the extract to support your answer.   (2)
(v)   From your study of the history of Northern Ireland, why do you think the British government introduced Direct Rule in 1972?   (2)

3. SHORT-ANSWER QUESTIONS (20 marks)

Answer TEN of the following questions. Each is worth 2 marks.

(i)   Mention **two** types of primary source a historian can use.   (2)
(ii)   Name **two** types of tomb from Neolithic Ireland.   (2)
(iii)   Mention **two** types of dwelling place from Celtic Ireland.   (2)
(iv)   Explain why cattle were so important to the Celts.   (2)
(v)   Give **two** important effects that the arrival of the *Normans* had on Ireland.   (2)
(vi)   Name **two** of the stages involved in the training of a knight during the Middle Ages.   (2)
(vii)   Explain **two** of the following terms relating to towns in the Middle Ages: *Curfew; Guild; Toll; Charter.*   (2)

(viii) During the Middle Ages what was the *Black Death*? (2)

(ix) Give **two** reasons why the Renaissance began in Italy. (2)

(x) Name **one** Renaissance sculptor and **one** of his works.
Sculptor:
Work: (2)

(xi) Mention **two** developments in Science **or** Medicine during the Renaissance. (2)

(xii) Give **two** reasons why many people thought that the Catholic Church was in need of reform in the early 16th century. (2)

(xiii) Name **one** religious reformer whom you have studied and **one** of his major beliefs.
Reformer:
Belief: (2)

(xiv) Mention **two** effects of the Reformation in Europe during the period 1517 to 1648. (2)

(xv) Give **two** reasons why the population of Britain increased so greatly during the first half of the 19th century. (2)

(xvi) Mention **two** reasons why *Sinn Féin* won the 1918 general election. (2)

(xvii) Name **two** parties that formed part of the *First Inter-Party* government, 1948–51. (2)

(xviii) What country lost land as a result of the Munich Conference, September 1938? (2)

(xix) Explain why the signing of the *Nazi-Soviet Non-Aggression Pact* caused great surprise in Europe in 1939. (2)

(xx) During World War II, what was *Operation Barbarossa*? (2)

ANSWER THE FOLLOWING QUESTIONS, 4, 5 AND 6, IN A SEPARATE ANSWER BOOK

4. PEOPLE IN HISTORY (40 marks)

Answer A and B

A. Select **one** of the people described below. Write about that person.

(i) An archaeologist working on a dig. (20)

(ii) A monk in a medieval monastery. (20)

(iii) A native of a land discovered by Europeans during the Age of Exploration. (20)

B. Select **one** of the people described below. Write about that person.

(i) A supporter of the government describes how revolution broke out in America **or** France **or** Ireland during the period, 1770–1815. (20)

(ii) A republican during the War of Independence in Ireland, 1919–21. (20)

(iii) A member of the Nazi party describes how Hitler came to power in Germany. (20)

5. PLANTATIONS IN IRELAND (30 marks)

Source D Source E

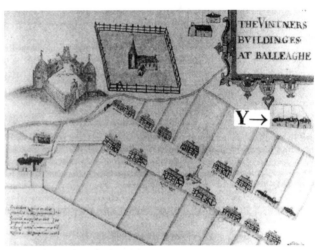

A. Study Source D, which is an illustration by Lucas de Heere (c.1575) of a civil woman from the Pale and a Gaelic Irishman.

    (i)   From the picture, give **one** piece of evidence to suggest that the artist felt that the Gaelic Irish were uncivilised. (2)

    (ii)   What was *the Pale*? (2)

    (iii)   Explain why the English began a policy of plantation in Ireland. (4)

B. Study Source E which is a drawing of the Vintners' settlement at Bellaghy and answer the questions that follow.

    (i)   Why did the settlers build a castle? (2)

    (ii)   From the picture, give **one** piece of evidence to suggest that the native Irish lived in the houses marked Y. (2)

    (iii)   Mention a British ruler who ordered that a plantation be carried out in Ireland. (2)

C. (i)   Give the name of **one** of the plantations that you have studied and write about the effects of that plantation on **two** of the following:

    (a)   Political control.

    (b)   Culture and customs.

    (c)   Religion. (2 x 8)

6. Answer **two** of the following questions, **A, B, C, D.** (60 marks)

A. FROM FARM TO FACTORY: SOCIAL CHANGES IN EIGHTEENTH- AND NINETEENTH-CENTURY BRITAIN

(i)   Mention **two** disadvantages of the Open Field System of farming.   (4)

(ii)   Name **one** improvement during the Industrial Revolution that you associate with each of **three** of the following:

James Hargreaves; James Watt; Abraham Darby; Edmund Cartwright; Richard Arkwright. (6)

(iii)   Write an account of **two** of the following:

(a)   Improvements in farming methods during the Agricultural Revolution.

(b)   Efforts to improve working conditions in the textile mills and the coal mines.

(c)   Living conditions for workers in the industrial towns.

(d)   Improvements in transport during the Industrial Revolution.   (2 x 10)

B. POLITICAL DEVELOPMENTS IN TWENTIETH-CENTURY IRELAND

(i)   **Events in Ireland 1900–1914**

Match each item in column A, (1)–(6) with its corresponding item in column B, (a)–(f).

You need not write out the full text in your answer book – just the correct number and letter.

Column A	Column B
1. Sir Edward Carson 2. Arthur Griffith 3. John Redmond 4. Herbert Asquith 5. The Irish Volunteers 6. James Larkin	(a) Home Rule politician (b) British political leader (c) Howth gun-running (d) Leader during the 1913 Strike and Lockout (e) Sinn Féin leader (f) Unionist leader in Ireland

(ii)   Give **two** reasons why many people in Ireland opposed the Treaty signed with Great Britain in December 1921.   (4)

(iii)   Write an account of **two** of the following:

(a)   The Blueshirts

(b)   Relations between the Irish government and the British government during the 1930s.

(c)   The 1960s in the Republic of Ireland.

(d)   Life in Northern Ireland during World War II.

(e)   The Civil Rights Movement in Northern Ireland.   (2 x 10)

C. SOCIAL CHANGE IN TWENTIETH-CENTURY IRELAND

(i)   Mention **two** changes that have occurred in agriculture since 1945.   (4)

(ii)   'The status of women in Irish society has improved greatly during the last 50 years.' Do you agree? Give **three** pieces of evidence to support your answer. (6)

(iii)   Write an account of how communications have changed in Ireland since 1945. (10)

(iv)   Write about the major changes that have occurred in the ways people spend their leisure time since 1945.   (10)

D. INTERNATIONAL RELATIONS IN THE TWENTIETH CENTURY

(i)   Give **one** reason why fascism became popular in Italy during the 1920s.   (2)

(ii)   Explain **two** of the following terms relating to Benito Mussolini and Italy: The March on Rome, 1922; The Blackshirts; The Lateran Treaty, 1929; The Rome-Berlin Axis, 1936.   (4)

(iii)   Write an account of **one** of the following:

    (a)   The Battle of Britain, 1940.

    (b)   The Battle of Stalingrad, 1942–43.

    (c)   The Allied landings in Normandy, 1944.   (12)

(iv)   *Please choose Topic 1 or 2 or 3 below.*

Topic 1 **The rise of the Superpowers**

(a)   Explain why the Cold War began after World War II.   (4)

(b)   Name **one** of the major crises of the Cold War and write an account of its effects on relations between the USA and the USSR.   (8)

or

Topic 2 **Moves towards European unity**

(a)   Why was there much support for the idea of European unity after World War II?   (4)

(b)   Write an account of the main events that have happened in the movement towards European unity after 1957.   (8)

or

Topic 3 **African and Asian nationalism**

(a)   In a **named** African or Asian country, mention **one** leader who led the movement towards independence.   (2)

(b)   Mention the colonial power that controlled the country that you have named.   (2)

(c)   Write an account of the independence struggle in that country after World War II.   (8)

JUNIOR CERTIFICATE EXAMINATION, 2002

HISTORY — HIGHER LEVEL

(180 Marks)

TUESDAY, 11 JUNE — AFTERNOON, 2.00 – 4.30

Answer *all* questions, **1**, **2** and **3** in the appropriate spaces on the examination paper.

1. **PICTURES** (15 marks)
    Study the pictures A, B1, B2 and C which accompany this paper and then answer the
    following questions.

    (*a*) **PICTURE A**

    Picture A shows a reconstruction of a crannóg at Craggaunowen, Co. Clare.

      (i)   Why do you think reconstructions such as the one shown in the picture
    were made?

    ....

    ....   (1)

(ii)   Identify **two** defensive features of the crannóg.

....

.... (2)

(iii)   "The walls of the houses on the crannóg were built using a method called <u>wattle and daub</u>."

Explain each of the words, <u>wattle</u> and <u>daub</u>.

Wattle:..

....

Daub:..

.... (2)

(*b*) **PICTURE B1 AND B2**

*Picture B1 shows the major leaders of the USSR at the official opening of the Moscow–Volga canal in 1936. The person marked **X** is Stalin, who ruled the USSR from 1928 until 1953. Picture B2 is the same picture after it was changed, on Stalin's orders, in 1939.*

B1

B2

(i) Why would political leaders consider it important to be photographed on an occasion such as that seen in picture B1?

....

.... (1)

(ii) Basing your answer on pictures B1 and B2, give **one** reason why the historian cannot always rely on visual sources.

....

.... (2)

(iii) Is picture B1 a primary source **or** a secondary source of information for the historian? Briefly explain your answer.

....

.... (2)

(c) **PICTURE C**

Picture C is a map that shows population change in Ireland between 1926 and 1961.

(i) Name **one** of the counties south of the border which had an increase in population during the period, 1926–1961.

.... (1)

(ii) Between 1954 and 1961 which year had the highest annual emigration from Northern Ireland?

.... (1)

(iii)   Name the **only** county in Northern Ireland where population fell during
        the period, 1926–1961.

        .... (1)

(iv)   Briefly explain why emigration from the Republic of Ireland was at its
        highest during the 1950s.

        ....
        ....
        .... (2)

C

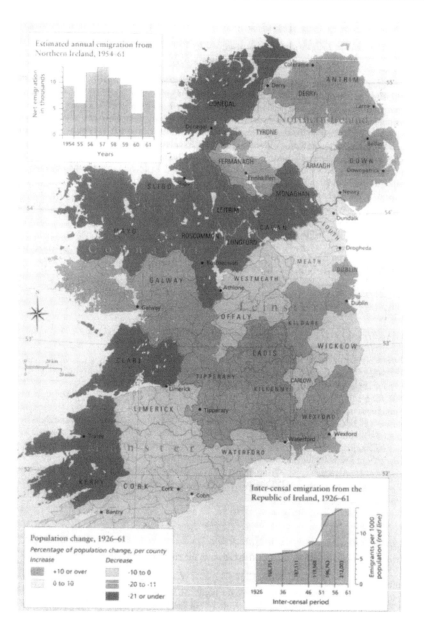

Estimated annual emigration from
Northern Ireland, 1954–61

Population change, 1926–61
Percentage of population change, per county

Inter-censal emigration from the
Republic of Ireland, 1926–61

2. **DOCUMENTS** (15 marks)

Read the two documents, **1** and **2**, which accompany this paper and then answer the following questions.

(a) **DOCUMENT 1**

This is the Solemn League and Covenant which was signed by Ulster Unionists on "Ulster Day", 28 September 1912.

The Solemn League and Covenant signed by Ulster Unionists on "Ulster Day", 28 September 1912

"Being convinced in our consciences that Home Rule would be disastrous to the material well-being of Ulster, as well as of the whole of Ireland, <u>subversive</u> of our civil and religious freedom, destructive of our citizenship, and <u>perilous</u> to the unity of the Empire, we whose names are underwritten, men of Ulster, loyal subjects of His Gracious Majesty King George V, humbly relying on the God Whom our fathers in the days of stress and trial confidently trusted, do hereby pledge ourselves in solemn Covenant throughout this our time of threatened calamity to stand by one another in defending for ourselves and our children our cherished position of equal citizenship in the United Kingdom and in using all means which may be found necessary to defeat the present conspiracy to set up a home rule parliament in Ireland.

And, in the event of such a parliament being forced upon us, we further and mutually pledge ourselves to refuse to recognise its authority. In sure confidence that God will defend the right, we hereto subscribe our names. And further, we individually declare that we have not already signed this Covenant. God Save the King."

- subversive = harmful
- perilous = dangerous

Source: A.C. Hepburn, "Ireland 1905–25. Volume 2 Documents and Analysis", p. 125.

(i) What did the signatories of the document "pledge to defend"?

.... (1)

(ii) What was "the present conspiracy" mentioned in the document?

....

.... (1)

(iii) Why do you think many people in Britain supported the Unionist campaign?

....

.... (1)

(iv) From the document identify **two** reasons why Unionists opposed Home Rule.

....

....

.... (2)

(v)   Apart from "Ulster Day", mention **two** actions taken by Ulster Unionists to resist Home Rule up to the outbreak of World War One.

....

....

....   (2)

(*b*) **DOCUMENT 2**

This is an extract from a speech on 7 January 1922 by Cathal Brugha during the debate in Dáil Éireann about the Anglo-Irish Treaty.

Extract from a speech by Cathal Brugha on 7 January 1922 during the debate in Dáil Éireann on the Anglo-Irish Treaty.

"Now Mr Griffith has referred to the difference between this Treaty of his and the alternative that we have as being only a <u>quibble</u>; and yet the English government is going to make war as they say they will, for a quibble. The difference is, to me, the difference that there is between a draught of water and a <u>draught</u> of poison. If I were to accept this treaty . . . I would, in my view, be committing national suicide; I would be breaking the national tradition that has been handed down to us through the centuries. We would be doing for the first time a thing that no generation thought of doing before – wilfully, voluntarily admitting ourselves to be British subjects, and taking the oath of allegiance voluntarily to an English king.

We are prepared to enter into an agreement, an association with the British Commonwealth of Nations as it is usually called, on the same or similar lines as that on which one business firm enters into association with another or several others . . . Now, by entry into a combination, no firm sacrifices its independence as a firm. We are prepared, on the same terms, to enter into an association with the British Commonwealth of Nations, and for the purpose of that combination we are prepared to recognise the English government as head of the combination . . . Now by entering into such arrangements we are not going into the British Empire: neither do we take any oath whatsoever; and there will be no representative of the British crown in the shape of a governor-general in Ireland."

- quibble = small detail
- draught = drink

Source: Dáil Éireann, Treaty Debates, pp. 325–34

(i)   In the view of Cathal Brugha, what was the difference between the Treaty and the alternative that he supported?

....

....   (1)

(ii)   What did Cathal Brugha mean when he spoke of "the national tradition that has been handed down to us through the centuries"?

....

....   (1)

(iii)   What example does Cathal Brugha use to explain his proposal?

....

....   (1)

(iv)   Who was he prepared to recognise "as head of the combination"?

....

....   (1)

(v)   Mention **two** reasons why he believed that an association with the British Commonwealth of Nations would have been better than the Treaty.

....

....

....   (2)

(vi)   From your knowledge of Irish history, mention **two** arguments put forward in **support** of the Treaty.

....

....

....   (2)

3.   **SHORT-ANSWER QUESTIONS** (20 marks)
     Answer TEN of the following questions. Each is worth 2 marks.

(i)   Explain **two** of the following terms as used by archaeologists:
         Artefact; Megalith; Midden; Post-hole.

....

....   (2)

(ii)   Name **two** methods used by archaeologists to try to date objects they find.

....   (2)

(iii)   Archaeologists sometimes describe the earliest Irish people as *hunter-gatherers*. What is meant by that term?

....

....   (2)

(iv)   In Celtic Ireland, what was *ogham*?

....   (2)

(v)   Explain **two** of the following terms from Celtic Ireland:
         Tuath; Fulacht fiadh; Souterrain; Tánaiste.

....

....   (2)

(vi)   In a medieval monastery, what was the *cloister*?

....   (2)

(vii)   Explain why there was a great demand for spices in Europe around the
        year 1500.

        ....
        ....   (2)

(viii) For what purposes were **two** of the following used during the Age of
        Exploration?
                Compass; Astrolabe; Portolan charts; Log and Line.

        ....
        ....   (2)

(ix)   Name the European country which discovered the sea route to India
        around the year 1500.

        ....   (2)

(x)   Mention **two** effects of the invention of the printing press.

        ....
        ....   (2)

(xi)   Why were patrons so important during the Renaissance?

        ....
        ....   (2)

(xii)   During the plantations in Ireland, explain a major difference between the
        Gaelic and the English systems of land ownership.

        ....
        ....   (2)

(xiii) Mention **two** effects of the American War of Independence on **either**
        France **or** Ireland.

        ....
        ....   (2)

(xiv)   Give **two** reasons why the Industrial Revolution began in Britain.

        ....
        ....   (2)

(xv)   Name the founder of the *Sinn Féin* party in 1905.
        ....   (2)

(xvi)   Mention **two** reasons why the 1916 Rising was a military failure.

        ....
        ....   (2)

(xvii) Explain **two** of the following terms relating to the War of Independence,
        1919–1921:
                Auxiliaries; The Squad; Flying Columns; Black and Tans.

        ....
        ....
        ....   (2)

(xviii) Briefly explain the importance of the Government of Ireland Act, 1920.

        ....
        ....   (2)

(xix)   Give **two** reasons why *fascism* became popular in Europe in the 1920s and 1930s.

....

....   (2)

(xx)   Mention **two** major changes that occurred in rural life in Ireland between 1945 and 2000.

....

....   (2)

ANSWER THE FOLLOWING QUESTIONS, 4, 5 AND 6, IN A SEPARATE ANSWER BOOK

4. **PEOPLE IN HISTORY** (40 marks)

Answer A and B

A. Select **one** of the people described below. Write about that person.

   (i)   A monk in a monastery in early Christian Ireland.   (20)

   (ii)   A named Renaissance painter **or** sculptor **who was not from Italy**.   (20)

   (iii)   A settler who received land in a **named** plantation in Ireland during the 16th or 17th century.   (20)

B. Select **one** of the people described below. Write about that person.

   (i)   A landlord in Ireland around the year 1850.

OR

            A factory owner **or** a mine owner in England around the year 1850.   (20)

   (ii)   An old woman describing changes in the role of women in Ireland between 1945 and 2000.   (20)

   (iii)   A political leader in the Republic of Ireland during the period 1949–1985.   (20)

5. **REFORMATION** (30 marks)
    SOURCE D
    Petrarch, Letter to a friend.

    "... Now I am living in France, in the Babylon of the West. Here reign the successors of the poor fishermen of Galilee; they have forgotten their origin. I am astounded, as I recall their predecessors, to see these men loaded with gold and clad in purple, boasting of the riches of princes and nations; to see luxurious palaces and heights crowned with fortifications ...

Instead of holy silence we find a criminal multitude . . . instead of soberness, drunken banquets; instead of pious pilgrimages, foul laziness; instead of the bare feet of the apostles, the war-horses of robbers fly past us, the horses decked in gold and fed on gold, soon to be shod with gold, if the lord does not check this slavish luxury."

(Source: J. H. Robinson, "Readings in European History", p. 502.)

SOURCE E

A contemporary picture of the massacre of Protestants in France on Saint Bartholomew's Day 1572.

SOURCE F

Extract from a letter from Catherine de Medici to her ambassador in Venice. She was the mother of the King of France at that time.

"The King is greatly troubled that in the heat of the moment certain Protestants were slain by the Catholics who remembered many evils, robberies and other wicked acts committed upon them . . . but now at last all is peaceful, so there is recognised only one king and one justice . . . because the King is determined, in view of the evils caused by differences of religions, to allow only his own religion."

A. Study Source D, which is an extract from a letter from Petrarch (1304–1374), a famous Renaissance writer, criticising the lifestyle of the Popes in the 14th century.

(i)   Who are "the successors of the poor fishermen of Galilee"? (2)

(ii)   Did the writer approve of what he saw? Mention **one** piece of evidence from the extract to support your answer. (2)

(iii)   Explain **three** of the following terms relating to the causes of the Reformation:
Simony; Nepotism; Absenteeism; Pluralism. (6)

B. (i)   Write down the name of a Protestant reformer whom you have studied. Outline **three** major differences between his beliefs and those of the Catholic Church. (6)

C. Source E is an artist's impression of the massacre of Protestants in France on Saint Bartholomew's Day, 1572. Source F is an extract from a letter from the mother of the King of France.

(i)   From Source E, give **two** pieces of evidence to show that the soldiers were acting very cruelly. (2)

(ii)   From Source F, how does Catherine de Medici explain the killings? (2)

(iii)   Write an account of **one** of the following topics:

       (a) The Council of Trent.
       (b) The Society of Jesus (The Jesuits).
       (c) Religious Wars in Europe, 1525–1648. (10)

6.   Answer **two** of the following questions **A, B, C** and **D**. (60 marks)

   A. OUR ROOTS IN ANCIENT CIVILISATION

   Select an ancient civilisation **<u>outside of Ireland</u>** that you have studied and answer the questions which follow.
   Please write the name of the ancient civilisation that you have selected at the top of your account.

(i)   Name **one** famous person associated with the civilisation that you have chosen. (2)

(ii)   Describe the house that a rich person lived in during the civilisation. (6)

(iii)   Write an account of **two** of the following in the civilisation:
       (a) Food and clothing; (b) Work, arts and crafts; (c) Burial customs.
       (2 x 8)

(iv)　In your opinion, what were the main achievements of that civilisation? (6)

B. THE MIDDLE AGES, 1100–1500

(i)　During the Middle Ages, what was *chivalry*?　(2)

(ii)　Mention **two** dangers faced by people living in towns during the Middle Ages.　(2)

(iii)　Explain **three** of the following terms relating to castles during the Middle Ages:

Turret; Moat; Keep; Portcullis; Bailey.　(6)

(iv)　Outline the main stages in the training of a craftsman in a medieval town.　(10)

(v)　Write an account of the life of a serf on a medieval manor.　(10)

C. POLITICAL DEVELOPMENTS IN TWENTIETH-CENTURY IRELAND

(i)　Give **two** reasons why the Home Rule party was unsuccessful in the 1918 General Election.　(4)

(ii)　In your answer-book, supply the missing words in the following sentences (1)–(6). You should number the words correctly but you need not re-write the sentences. **Do not answer this question on your examination paper.**

(1)　Sir James .... was the first Prime Minister of Northern Ireland.

(2)　The .... party was the largest party in Northern Ireland in the 1920s.

(3)　............ was the practice of dividing up electoral districts in order to give some political party an advantage.

(4)　The Prime Minister of Northern Ireland from 1963 until 1969 was Sir Terence ....

(5)　The Civil Rights Movement was set up to campaign for better conditions for the .... minority.

(6)　............ or imprisonment without trial was introduced by the Northern Ireland government in 1971.　(6)

(iii)　Write an account of **two** of the following:

(*a*)　James Larkin.
(*b*)　Cumann na nGaedheal in government, 1922–1932.

(c)   The Economic War, 1932–1938.

(d)   Life in Ireland during World War II, 1939–1945.

(e)   The First Inter-Party government, 1948–1951.   (2 x 10)

D. INTERNATIONAL RELATIONS IN THE TWENTIETH CENTURY

(i)   Mention **two** methods used by the Nazis to establish a dictatorship in Germany.   (4)

(ii)   In your answer-book, supply the missing words in the following sentences (1)–(6). You should number the words correctly but you need not re-write the sentences.
Do not answer this question on your examination paper.

     (1)   In 1936 German troops entered the ....

     (2)   In the same year Hitler and .... formed an alliance known as the Rome-Berlin Axis.

     (3)   In March 1939, Germany took over Austria in an event known as the ....

     (4)   At the Munich Conference the .... was given to Germany.

     (5)   The rest of .... was occupied by Germany in March 1939.

     (6)   The British Prime Minister, Neville Chamberlain, believed in a foreign policy known as ....   (6)

(iii)   Write an account of **one** of the following:

     (a)   Early German victories in World War II, September 1939–April 1940.

     (b)   The defeat of France, 1940.

     (c)   Life in Britain during World War II.   (10)

(iv)   *By May 1945, Germany had been completely crushed and had surrendered to the Allies.*

     In the light of the above statement, write an account of the reasons for the Allied victory.   (10)